Anyone Can Be Rich!

Anyone Can Be Rich!

A Psychiatrist Provides the Mental Tools to Build Your Wealth

Mark Tobak MD

ISBN: 1974582582
ISBN-13: 9781974582587

*To these learned and generous teachers, known by their writings and recordings:
Daniel Kahneman and the late Amos Tversky, who have scientifically
studied the misperceptions of our common sense;
Warren Buffett and Charlie Munger, who built a financial colossus through the
application of uncommon common sense and compounding and then shared
their wealth with their shareholders and their wisdom with the world; and
John C. Bogle, who operationalized the efficient market hypothesis
to work for anyone and everyone, if only they would listen.
Every idea in this book, in one way or another, I owe to them.*

It's no shame to be poor, but it's no great honor either.
—TEVYE THE MILKMAN, FIDDLER ON THE ROOF

I've been rich and I've been poor. Rich is better.
—SOPHIE TUCKER

Preface

I have been a practicing psychiatrist for more than twenty-five years. I have never earned a lot of money in any single year. But over the course of my life, I have approached, by the measure of the average American, the fringe of being comfortably rich. In time I will probably become comfortably rich. I will never be wealthy, but I don't care about that. It's the independence that is important to me, and that occurs with just a modicum of wealth.

Like most people born in the 1950s, I started off poor. Like Sophie Tucker in the second of my epigraph quotes, I have learned that rich is certainly better. Not worrying about the bills. Not worrying if the roof will leak when I can't afford to fix it. Not worrying about the car breaking down when I can't afford to repair or replace it. Not worrying about the costs of getting sick if I or a loved one should. I need not go on. We all know it's true.

Most of my life is spent with my patients. Very few are remotely rich. Most are just plain folks. Poor, working class, and middle class. One of my few wealthy patients asked me one day, "How many of your patients worry about money?" I replied frankly, "All of them." And I realized I was sitting in a room with the one other person with whom I spend a lot of time who does not worry about money. We watch over it, of course, but we don't worry about it.

I thought how wonderful it would be if more people knew how to get rich. Not quickly, with the winning lottery ticket so many of my patients pine for, but slowly and honestly over a lifetime. My goal in this book is to teach you to do just that with some simple ideas that are both old and venerable and others that are new but intuitive once you understand them. No stock tips. But an understanding of the human mind, money, markets, and life that can guide you there. I can assure you that nothing in this book will be difficult to understand. A little math. No tests. In the language of the streets, I just want to "wise you up." I have tried my best not to make it boring by using references and examples from our beloved popular culture. It may be uncomfortable at times, but only to the extent that giving up get-rich-quick dreams might be discomforting. Such dreams cause so much suffering over a lifetime and, in Robert Burns's timeless phrase, "leave us nought but grief and pain for promised joy."

One proviso and a disclaimer. I am not a financial consultant, and I do not give financial advice. This book is a guide to the management of your mind about your money. It is not an investment guide. For that I refer to you the sage advice of the expert mentors listed above and within and to the professionals, if duly vetted.

Contents

Introduction

Why would a psychiatrist write a book about getting rich? Could a psychiatrist truly be qualified? I pondered this question for some time before picking up a pen to write this book. I can marshal other credentials. I am a retired attorney—a brief career before going to medical school—so I know something about the law as it applies to money and people. I have also been a bellhop, a writer, a dishwasher, a postal worker, a garment-center floor boy, an assistant in a literary agency, and a short-order cook! Those jobs taught me things about money and people too. No matter what job I had, I always tried to save money and invest it in solid American companies, the heart and soul of growing rich. So, having invested since childhood, having made many mistakes in investing (some ongoing), and having researched and read the literature of finance and the psychology of investing, I feel I have learned a bit and have something to share about it. But the most important thing I have learned about successful investing and growing rich over a lifetime is that it can be surprisingly simple and certain. Anyone can do it. The barriers to doing it are really emotional and cognitive—in short, psychiatric! What I work at every day in my practice. You don't have to be smart, good looking, well connected, or well bred to grow rich. What keeps most people from ever accumulating wealth is not understanding money, not knowing how to manage and nurture it, not properly taming emotions about it, and not having a long-term approach to life. That is, not having what psychologists call a long time horizon where wealth is concerned.

Money is a tool, not a toy. If you learn the essential rules of using that tool properly, anyone can *slowly* grow rich over a lifetime. That's right—*slowly*. This is no get-rich-quick book. Those books and videos are scams. They tease and taunt you with impossible dreams. Reading this book will, among other things, help you to relinquish those dreams for a practical plan for wealth accumulation. It will help you get on the long but high road to the comforts and satisfactions of earned affluence. As Warren Buffett, the most accomplished investor in human history, has preached, "Take the high road; it's far less crowded."[1]

Before we begin, we should take some time to discuss greed and miserliness. Greed is rightly called a sin. It is the desire to possess more than one needs in material wealth. Greed was believed, in the ancient world of scarce resources, to inspire crime, robbery, thievery, scam, and manipulation. It is often presumed that the wealthy are, by definition, greedy and that you cannot acquire wealth without greed to inspire it. Honoré de Balzac is reputed to have said, "Behind every great fortune is a great crime." But the true quotation runs differently: "The secret of great fortunes without apparent cause is a crime forgotten, for it was properly done."[2]

Certainly we know of now-proud families whose fortunes were made through crime. It makes a tidy literary epigram to claim it as a universal. Surely it makes for a better movie or novel than a fortune accumulated through wise and steady work, which is, by definition, dull, nonliterary, and noncinematic. Almost everyone has seen *The Godfather*,[3] the iconic story of the rise of an immigrant crime family to staggering wealth and corruption. But there is no novel or film of the saga of Henry Ford, who, setting aside his politics, was a very great man who amassed a vast fortune while contributing enormously to the progress of the United States, revolutionizing manufacturing and transportation through assembly-line production of cars and trucks, and building a brand that survives to this day. Was he greedy or corrupt? Not according to any evidence I have seen. He paid his workers well and sold inexpensive and reasonably reliable cars. He established the Ford Foundation.

No movie biopic, just documentaries.

---

1 https://quotefancy.com/quote/931267/Warren-Buffett-Take -the-high-road-it's-far-less-crowded (accessed September 17, 2017)..

2 http://en.wikiquote.org/wiki/Honore_de_Balzac (accessed September 17, 2017).

3 *The Godfather*, Dir. Francis Ford Coppola, Paramount, 1972, Film.

Warren Buffett is, depending upon the day, the wealthiest or one of the wealthiest men in the world. One has never heard him called greedy. Why? He has made his money honestly. He has never lived ostentatiously. He has shared his wisdom and his money with the public. He is leaving most of his fortune to charity. His business partner, Charlie Munger, shares these same principles, and his writings and speeches offer a prescription for amassing wealth and not suffering enmity or the accusations of greed or corruption:

1. Acquire it through honest work.
2. Seek wealth to gain freedom and not to indulge yourself.
3. Get rich slowly, enjoy the process, and share the fruits.[4]

Wealth, appropriately employed, leads to better education for yourself, your children, and your grandchildren; improved health and longevity; access to quality health care; quality food; greater safety; and freedom from want for yourself and loved ones. For you to become wealthy does not mean someone else has to become poor. Prosperity is not a zero-sum game.

The wealthy are often portrayed in the mass media as cheap, mean, or miserly, like Mr. Potter in It's a Wonderful Life.[5] When someone gets rich, people will say, "He lived like a rat!" or "He squeezed that dollar!" But no one gets rich counting pennies or cheating waiters and cabbies. People also say, "They were lucky." Someone said that to Alan Jay Lerner's father about his son. He answered, "Yes, the harder he works the luckier he gets!"[6]

People often hate the rich, hate the people who "make it," because they are envious. Why wouldn't they be? As Charlie Munger explains, envy is powerful enough to make at least two of the Ten Commandments.[7] But you won't find envy in the

---

4   Peter D. Kaufman, ed., Poor Charlie's Almanack: The Wit and Wisdom of Charles T. Munger, Expanded Third Edition (Marceline, MO: Walsworth Publishing Company, 2005), p.465..

5   It's a Wonderful Life, Dir. Frank Capra, Liberty Films, 1946, Film.

6   Alan Jay Lerner, The Street Where I Live (New York: Norton, 1978).

7   Charles T. Munger, "The Psychology of Human Misjudgment," in Poor Charlie's Almanack: The Wit and Wisdom of Charles T. Munger, Expanded Third Edition, ed. Peter D. Kaufman (Marceline, MO: Walsworth Publishing Company, 2005), and https://www.hb.org/the-psychology-of-human-misjudgment-by-charles-t-munger/(accessed September 17, 2017).

psychology texts! Certainly, the politically correct message of the noble poor and the decadent, greedy rich makes a good story line. And it sells to a wide audience. There are many more poor than rich. Money can be misused by either group, rich or poor. And there are good and bad in both groups, as in all of humanity. I remember a young patient many years ago, a gifted man from a poor family, who was shocked that, after his graduation, so many top-level organizations full of wealthy people courted and nurtured him, treating him with kindness and generosity. Meanwhile, some of the street people in his neighborhood tried to hustle and even rob him. He was dumbfounded by the contrast. The media had fed him a politically correct message about poor and rich, but reality was teaching him something more nuanced.

Understandably, the media are performing their mission to "afflict the comfortable and comfort the afflicted."[8] The media has no room for the self-made millionaire who toiled long and hard or the angry lout who throws away success with both hands and ends up poor. Neither is a story that will sell.

I once worked for a literary agency that received a letter from a naïve would-be writer who asked why there were no novels about honest people who worked hard and achieved much over a long life. Answer: No story. No hook. No hero. No villain. A story requires a heroic lead, beaten and chained by cruel fate and cruel adversaries, who, through a deft story line, throws off the shackles, defeats the adversaries, and wins the day. That is not merely a rule for novelists; it embraces all the media all the time.

There are other myths about money. That being poor is noble and that suffering poverty is ennobling. This may be true in song and fable: "We ain't got a barrel of money, maybe we're ragged and funny, but we'll travel along, singing a song, side by side."[9] The Bible teaches about the rich man and the kingdom of heaven. But nowadays the waiting room to the next world may well be a hospital, a long-term-care facility, or a

---

8   https://www.poynter.org/news/today-media-history-mr-dooley-job-newspaper-comfort-afflicted-and-afflict-comfortable (accessed September 17, 2017).

9   Harry M. Woods, *Side By Side* (New York: Shapiro Bernstein & Co., 1927).

nursing home. If you have not planned and invested for your old age, your quality of late life may well be poor, but it will hardly be ennobling.

We do not live in a world of scarcity today. We live in a world of abundance, at least in the United States. I firmly believe that anyone who works earnestly and unceasingly in life, whether worker, professional, or entrepreneur, can build enough wealth to become rich over a lifetime by applying the principles espoused in this book, without greed or miserliness. The principles are not mine. I have borrowed them all from the great minds of psychology and finance. I will name the great minds throughout the book and urge you to read them in the originals, as I have condensed and simplified their ideas in attempting to make them available to the widest possible readership.

A word about self-destructiveness. Fortunes large and small have been made and lost. In my life I have witnessed wealth and inheritances squandered on bad habits and addictions, lost through bad marriages, divorces, high living, and indolence. I have seen large personal-injury awards and settlements frittered away, leaving people both disabled and dependent. Many successful entrepreneurs have lost their fortunes while seeking larger ones, begging Warren Buffett's question, "Why would you risk what you need and have for what you don't need?"[10] But people do.

The greatest discoveries of modern economics did not come from economics. They came from science and psychology: the work of Daniel Kahneman and Amos Tversky, whom I introduce later in this book. They proved that humans are not economic computers made of meat who weigh rationally what they do. We are emotionally and cognitively fragile, evolved creatures whose archaic hardwiring can misguide us in how we deal with our finances and our futures. If I can provide some mental software to help your finances and your future, this book will have accomplished its purpose.

---

10 Warren Buffett speaking before MBA students at the University of Maryland, quoted by Ben Carlson in "Don't Try to Get Rich Twice," at awealthofcommonsense.com/2016/11/don't-try-to-get-rich-twice/(accessed September 17, 2017).

This book is divided into five parts:

Part I examines how people can be irrational about money. The human mind is evolved and not wired from scratch like a computer.

Part II teaches how to manage the evolved mind to grow money into wealth despite human irrationality.

Part III explains how to keep money from those who might take it from you and includes a faux Bible story about growing and keeping money, with characters and ideas to emblazon it in your memory and help you pass it along to others.

Part IV is an introduction to my beloved teachers, the world's greatest investors, whose lives, writings, and teachings will expand your understanding of money, markets, and life.

Part V, for the bold and daring, is a discussion of how one might prosper buying individual stocks, which I cannot recommend as a practice.

PART I

Your Mind and Your Money

CHAPTER 1

Common Sense, Not So Common

So much of our lives are lived with plain common sense, popularly called "horse sense." Indeed, we share much of the wiring for common sense with our fellow animals. No one needs to teach us or other primates to fear snakes. It is instinctive. Our primate relatives—monkeys and chimps—are terrified of snakes, even if they have never seen one before. It is hardwired, so to speak. Even the simple pigeon fears rubber snakes on an urban window ledge. Respect for heights is common sense too. Dogs and cats know from what heights they can safely jump. A horse will balk at a jump it believes it cannot negotiate safely.

Small numbers can be handled with common sense. A dog knows if he gets one treat or two and will wait for the second if he is accustomed to it. But dogs cannot count, and the famous Clever Hans, the counting horse, was a clever fraud. His trainer tipped him off. Humans can count if they are taught to. But not all of us can learn to do it well or handle mathematics beyond the rudimentary. Those who can are sometimes the absent-minded professors of academia, whose common sense is often suspect.

However, two great professors of psychology, Daniel Kahneman and the late Amos Tversky, discerned, through brilliant theorizing and clever experimentation, that our common sense and our thoughtful selves are two different systems in the brain, which they call System One and System Two. Kahneman entitled his popular book, *Thinking Fast and Slow*, for System One and System Two. System One is close to what I am calling common sense—quick and dirty. System Two is, as Kahneman notes, slow and thoughtful, the system we need to take math tests and write reports and papers, to really figure something out. Let's call it "book smarts" or "uncommon sense." These two systems often don't produce the same results, particularly when it comes to science, technology, engineering, and mathematics, nowadays known by the acronym STEM. To understand money and markets, you need both.[1]

The popular TV sitcom *Big Bang Theory* has endured for years plotting comic collisions between common sense–filled and street-smart Penny and her book-smart, nerdy STEM friends.

Funny until it's not. The best real-life example of book smarts smashing head-on into common sense is the fate of Long-Term Capital Management, a now-defunct hedge-fund-management firm composed of the finest STEM minds in finance. They amassed billions through sophisticated trading with borrowed money until they lost everything, nearly toppling world markets, in a failure of plain old common sense. Common sense says that improbable, horrible, and "unpredictable" things do happen, and they did happen in the successive Asian and Russian financial crises. As Mike Tyson wisely said, "Everyone has a plan 'til they get punched in the mouth."[2]

We can all agree that it is vastly easier to get by in the world with common sense than to try to always be book smart and perform the mental equivalent of heavy lifting all day long. And I won't ask you to do much mental heavy lifting in this book. Some very wise people have, gratefully, already done it for us. You can download their wisdom into your common sense without much trouble as long as you're willing to give up your pride in a few fixed ideas and perhaps be surprised and awakened to a new common sense about money and markets. Common sense is malleable.

After all, it was common sense in the year 1000 that the world was flat. Common sense now says it is round, informed by science and exploration. Common sense in 1900 said automobiles would never be safe or reliable and would never replace the horse. "Get a horse!" was a frequent taunt to the stranded motorist. Today's common sense is that cars are highly reliable and horseback riding is an elite but dangerous

---

1 Daniel Kahneman, *Thinking Fast and Slow* (New York: Farrar, Straus and Giroux, 2011).

2 https://www.brainyquote.com/quotes/quotes/m/miketyson382439.html.(accessed September 17,2017)

sport. Common sense in 1928 said stocks could only go up. Common sense in 1930 said stocks could only go down. Common sense in 1944 said smoking was chic, attractive, and pleasurable. Now common sense says it's dangerous, disease causing, and addictive. Common sense in 1800 said man and the animals were created by an all-knowing God in his infinite wisdom. Common sense in 2017 says we live in an evolved world that has been growing and changing for millions of years, though a beneficent God may well watch over it.

So this is the beginning of a tour of the ways in which common sense defeats most people's efforts—and can defeat your efforts—to become rich over time. Commonsense impressions gleaned from life and the media about money and wealth can fool you. As Obi-Wan Kenobi tells Luke Skywalker in *Star Wars: A New Hope*: "Your senses can fool you. Don't trust them."[3]

Look around the world, and you see rich and poor and think that it was ever thus. Yes, "the poor are always with [us]."[4] In a sense this is true. There have always been rich and poor. But the invisible reality is *fortunes rise and fall.*

Many rich people were born poor or middle class, and some poor people once had money and blew it. Think of the many people who win the lottery and file for bankruptcy two years later.[5] Also, many people who appear to be rich have little actual wealth—just a lot of stuff they like to display. Some people who lead conventional middle-class lives are worth millions but do not spend ostentatiously. Finally, there are the scions of wealth who have spent their elders' fortunes, were swindled or cajoled or divorced out of money, or lost it trying to spin it into a larger fortune. Building wealth involves recognizing that basic rules routinely applied dutifully over a long life, beginning when you are very young, can make you or anyone else rich.

---

3 *Star Wars: Episode IV-A New Hope*, Dir. George Lucas, Lucasfilm Ltd, 1977, Film.

4 Matthew 26:11.

5 https://www.nytimes.com/interactive/2016/01/14/us/lottery-winners-whose-lives-were-ruined.html (accessed September 17,2017).

If you approach gambling and lotteries with unalloyed common sense, you might think that betting winners could make you rich, if only you could find them. "A dollar and a dream."

Winners in ads and the news invite you to join in and take your share. That invitation is reinforced by our naïve search for pleasure, the dopamine rush in the brain we all seek, whether it's from a good meal, a personal triumph, a material acquisition, or romantic love.

Twice in my life, I have found cash in the street. Less than twenty dollars each time. As a successful professional, I make much more than that every working hour of every day. But I don't remember any of that earned money. It is lost in the great pot of income and expense. I will remember that found money always: the place, the weather, and the act of bending to pick it up. (There was no one around to return it to.) Why? Because found or stolen money provides a dopamine rush of pleasure that earned money cannot. Stolen fruit tastes sweeter. That dopamine rush is highly addictive.

The briefer and more intense the pleasure, the more we remember and want to replicate it. Found money is a sudden, brief, unearned thrill. In *American Graffiti*, directed by George Lucas of *Star Wars* fame, a group of teenage boys observe a stunning blonde, a young Suzanne Somers, as she drives by in a Thunderbird. Seen only for an instant, she is a greater dopamine rush than if she had paused, spoken, or stepped out of the car.[6] Lucas understands the human brain and the cinematic power of brief and intense imagery. This awareness is much like that of Michael Curtiz, the unsung director of *Casablanca*, who rebuffed critiques: "I make it go so fast no one notices."[7]

Exciting money is fast money. Watching paint dry, grass grow, or water boil is dull and boring. But actual wealth grows like grass: slowly, surely, and certainly. That growth doesn't fit how we have evolved to want things. When do we want money?

---

6 *American Graffiti*, Dir. George Lucas, Lucasfilm Ltd, 1973, Film.

7 *Casablanca*, Dir. Michael Curtiz, Warner Brothers, 1942, Film.
Aljean Harmetz, *Round Up the Usual Suspects: The Making of "Casablanca"—Bogart, Bergman, and World War II* (New York: Hyperion, 1992).

Now, of course. When do we really want it? Yesterday. Even the word "wealth" is a bore. "Money" is exciting.

That's why everyone loves a good heist movie. Will these bold, fascinating, gorgeous criminals get away with all that money? Will they disappear into some tropical paradise and lead lives of leisure and pleasure with their ill-gotten gains while middle-income detectives gnash their teeth in disgust?

Why are so many lottery winners on TV? It's just the same story endlessly retold. Why don't TV journalists go from house to house in elite precincts and interview self-made millionaires, who built businesses and factories from scratch and became wealthy through decades of eighty-hour workweeks? Because it does not appeal to our animal nature—no dopamine rush. So it is not, in a journalistic sense, a story. Common sense tells you it is not.

Our animal nature seeks a quick and easy buck. We are more easily drawn to gambling tables and lotteries than to school or work. And the desire to gamble can be dangerously reinforced by a chance win or, preferably and more likely, tamed by bitter experience. All but a few gamblers lose, and those who briefly win usually lose it all back. The misguided who return again and again are, at various turns, addicted, addled, or entertained. The largest portion of the gambling public is, unsurprisingly, poor. There is no rational reason to take a bad bet, especially if there are good bets to be had. But animal models of reinforcement have proven that we respond most regularly to random and unpredictable wins—they keep us coming back for more.

Just as insidious and seductive as gambling is the lure of markets. Common sense coupled with the search for pleasure beckon you to buy a rising stock, sell it at a profit, repeat this endlessly, and grow rich. It is intuitive. It is common sense. It is promised joy.

It does not work! No one can reliably predict the short-term rise or fall of any stock or the direction of the market. No one.

I once knew a very book-smart fellow who discovered the raucously overconfident market pundits of financial TV and dutifully followed their every recommendation until he was ruined in the space of a few years. Media pundits are rarely tracked or evaluated for predictive accuracy, and if they are, they are most frequently wrong. But they all observe the celebrity wisdom of never apologize, never explain and just go on to the next overconfident prediction.

Confidence will always outshine accuracy in the broadcast media. Our animal natures lead us to trust the confident and distrust the anxious and self-effacing. Any hint of doubt in a leader can undermine his or her power.

If you are training an animal, you must display total confidence and control. If you have never been to a horse barn or a horse show, it is educative to watch a seemingly fearless (no one is actually fearless) one-hundred-pound woman in total control of a two-thousand-pound horse. Watch a thirteen-pound Cairn Terrier—Toto from the *Wizard of Oz*—tell any animal of any weight who's boss.[8] In legal practice I learned that confident, guiltless liars are more convincing than worried, anxious truth-tellers. Look at politics.

The best example of irresistible human surrender to brazen confidence is a comedy bit by the great Buddy Hackett, my father's favorite comedian. Buddy loved to tell the story of the racetrack tout who, miserable, disheveled, and dressed in tatters, insistently promises you the name of the winner of the next race. And you listen, compulsively, defying the very evidence before you that this man knows less than nothing! Indeed, you forget, for the moment, that no one knows the winner of the next race.

So if we cannot look to the pundits, what about the stockbrokers? Woody Allen famously said, "A stockbroker is someone who invests other people's money until it is all gone."[9] Again, no one can predict the direction of a stock or the markets in general

---

8 *Wizard of Oz*, Dir. Victor Fleming, Metro-Goldwyn-Mayer, 1939, Film.

9 https://quotefancy.com/quote/949703/woody-allen-stockbroker-is-someone-who-invests-other-people-s-money-until-it-is-all (accessed September 17, 2017).

in the short term. The very best investors will tell you that. So are the brokers and pundits lying or just kidding themselves? It really doesn't matter. Trading stocks frequently is a fool's errand. It makes the financial industry rich and the trader poor. There is a famous book, published in 1940, *Where Are the Customers' Yachts?: Or, a Good, Hard Look at Wall Street* by Fred Schwed.[10] The title is based on the naïve question of a bumpkin investor observing the luxurious yachts of the brokers and bankers in the harbors of lower Manhattan. Of course, the customers do not own yachts, though they have paid dearly for those admired by our bumpkin.

All academic research studies of investing and markets confirm that frequent trading is a road to ruin for the average investor. Across the general public, female investors have better results than males, on average. Why? They trade less often. They are not overconfident. Even the frequent traders who do "make a killing" may not keep it—just like the gamblers in Vegas who, if they continue to play with the odds against them, lose their winnings to the house.

And what about those hedge funds run by genius investors with top-flight tech and intellectual support out of academia? Surely, there have been breathtaking successes. But Warren Buffett put the industry to the test in a ten-year-long bet: he offered $1 million, proceeds to a charity of the winner's choice, to any combination of hedge-fund investments that, after fees, could beat an S&P 500 index fund, the most widely accepted measure of the broad market. A prominent hedge-fund manager took the bet. Nine years later, he admitted defeat after it was statistically impossible for him to win.[11] Warren Buffett does not knowingly make bad bets.

What, then, is predictable? The slow, inexorable, uneven, rocky, long-term, compounding rise of the financial markets. That is predictable. That is historical truth and historically inevitable. World markets, over time, will inevitably grow. Especially here in the United States. Just as the population grows, technology grows, and the world's wealth grows. Getting an early start on that gravy train is the surest road to wealth.

---

10   Fred Schwed, *Where Are the Customers' Yachts?: Or, a Good, Hard Look at Wall Street* (Hoboken, NJ: Wiley, 2006).

11   https://www.bloomberg.com/view/articles/2017/-05-03/why-i-lost-my-bet-with-warren-buffett(accessed September 17, 2017).

It should be obvious. It is to a wise few. It is uncommon common sense. My goal is to make it common sense for you.

Unalloyed common sense does not tell us to think rationally and mathematically. It does tell us to follow the crowd—the actions and behaviors of other people. We like to submerge ourselves in crowds and lose our egos in the comfort of knowing we have their support. We are in the in-crowd. One of the most important books for the understanding of markets is Charles Mackay's *Extraordinary Popular Delusions and the Madness of Crowds*.[12] Published in 1841, Mackay's book chronicled the tulip mania of seventeenth-century Holland, the single most compelling example of manifest follow-the-crowd stupidity ever, the best example of "it seemed like a good idea at the time." Mackay describes, in the language of his day, the mad frenzy of bidding over tulip bulbs, the must-have Apple iPhones of their day, newly arrived in Holland. Prices rose so high that a single bulb could buy an entire house.

Then, suddenly, the market collapsed: prices plummeted, and the bulbs were nearly worthless. As Mackay famously wrote, "Men, it has been well said, think in herds; it will be seen that they go mad in herds, while they only recover their senses slowly, and one by one." Remember the dot-com craze of our own era.

Who knew their Mackay then?

So, if we are natural herd animals and crowd followers capable of lemming-like behaviors, what does it say to us when we watch other people winning lotteries on TV news or joyous masses at casino tables winning on TV commercials? The human mind cannot distinguish real experience from media experience. If others are betting and winning, so will we. That's why publicists hire clappers at concerts and producers add laugh tracks to TV sitcoms. If we hear clapping, we clap. If we hear laughter, we laugh. If we see winning bettors, we will bet.

---

12 Charles Mackay, *Extraordinary Popular Delusions and the Madness of Crowds* (Mineola, NY: Dover Publications, 2005).

We follow crowds, but we love individuals more. I was once lucky enough to dine with the Nobel Prize–winning author Isaac Bashevis Singer. He told me something I will never forget. "You cannot deal with masses in literature." I did not fully understand what he meant. I was just over twenty. But time has made it clear to me. Movies, which I confess I love more than literature, made it clear. All of our most beloved movies are about individual people. Think of just two evergreens: *Casablanca* and *Star Wars*.

Both of them are about war, but not really about war as much as about the lives of a few people, whom we quickly learn to love dearly and who are caught up in war. This war is not of their own making, but it is one they have to fight at the risk of their lives to save the world or, in *Star Wars*, the galaxy. Talk about powerful! But the point is there are countless wars and countless war movies, and people die, but you don't remember them. Yet you do remember these two movies and are moved by them because you know and love the individuals: Rick and Ilsa, Luke, Han, Leia, and Obi-Wan. They are our dear friends, we care about them, and we want them to survive and succeed. Individuals matter to us, and masses don't. A quote perhaps misattributed to Stalin, "A single death is a tragedy; a million deaths is a statistic."[13]

It's not a far stretch to realize that people feel the same way about individual stocks as they do about individual people. It's common sense that individual stocks would matter to us more than the broad stock market. The market is just a statistic! Picking stocks is where the real action should be! But if you bring that commonsense sensibility to the market and pick individual stocks without the wisdom and insight of a Buffett or a Munger, you are taking a risky bet. Charlie Munger teaches never to take a risky bet when there are good bets to be had. In his metaphor, he wants to shoot fish in a barrel after the water has been drained out.[14]

It is not common sense that betting on the broad market is a sure bet and betting on an individual stock is a risky one because we want to pick our own stocks, and we want our stocks to win. It is a standard psychological principle that once you

---

13 https://www.psychologytoday.com/blog/life-autopilot/201003/why-is-the-death-one-million-statistic (accessed September 17, 2017).

14 www.marketwatch.com/story/5things-ive-learned-from-charlie-munger-2017-01-04?mg=prod/accounts-mw (accessed September 17, 2017).

pick or buy something, it becomes special in your eyes. The lucky number you pick in the lottery is a sure winner. People buy more lottery tickets when they pick their own numbers. The car you chose is better than your neighbor's. The house you chose is better than your friend's. The stock you bought is better and is going to go up because you bought it.

Nature wants us to think we are special and lucky, and such thinking distorts our objectivity and our common sense. Nature imbues every creature with more than a measure of confidence. Without confidence it will not survive and reproduce. If nature did not give us each the confidence to face the day, if we all retreated in search of safety, we would all be shut-ins hiding at home in a safe place, a personal and evolutionary dead end. Observe your fellow humans: the bold and the confident thrive, enjoy life, and succeed, marry, and reproduce. Shyness and fear may keep you safe for a time, but they never grant success. In computer-modeled animal worlds fraught with deathtraps, bold "creatures" die more frequently than timid ones. Nature does not care about that. Nature has many more creatures. Nature seeks only the survival of the best adapted. Nature, in this regard, is more like an evil dictator than a benevolent god. Dictators don't care how many soldiers or subjects they lose as long as the battle is won.

As an individual, you have to care about yourself, of course, because you are merely you, and if you hurt, you hurt, and if you die, it's over. But confidence, even cockiness, especially in youth, is a birthright. We see that very cockiness and confidence in spades when people are gambling and when they buy and then proudly tout their stocks. But the stock does not know *you* own it. The stock couldn't care that you own it. The stock does not care what you paid for it or if you sell it or keep it. But still people get a feeling about their stock and want it to succeed. It is a Wall Street maxim that one should never fall in love with a stock.

But everybody wants to be a winner, and you can become a winner by picking winners. We get into a school, and we want our school to win. We join a firm or a company, and we want it to succeed. We pick a team, and we root for it. We pick a star player on a team, and our children wear the jersey and root and feel they participate in the star's success. We're people, this is what we do, and it's fine as long as you don't bring this kind of "common sense" crowd following, friendship making and magical thinking to the stock market. Because there you will, with rare exception, be punished for it.

Charlie Munger teaches that to succeed in markets, you need to employ the wisdom of science and math, which, regrettably, very few people have the patience to study and learn. But even if you don't know science and math in depth, you can learn some broad principles, and they can inform your common sense.

It took civilization until little more than one hundred years ago to awaken to the reality of evolution. Evolution—the idea that we evolved over eons of time from the simplest chemicals to organic compounds to primitive life forms and, ultimately, through reptiles, mammals, and primates to us—is not intuitive, not common sense and not even accepted by all people everywhere today, even highly intelligent and educated people. It is a hard-won concept, and it took a great and patient man who questioned his every assumption to work it out—Charles Darwin.

What can Darwinian evolution teach us about markets? That 99 percent of all the species that have ever inhabited the earth are gone—extinct. If you bet on the tyrannosaurus rex, the king of the dinosaurs, you lost. Dead. If you're a born contrarian and bet on the dodo, you lost. Dead. But if you bet on life, life in general, you have won big time! Life is still here, abundant, ever changing, and still evolving.

So let's apply Darwinian evolution to the stock market. Look at the great stocks of yesteryear. General Motors—the titan of which it was said in the Eisenhower years, "As goes General Motors, so goes the nation"—went bankrupt and wiped out common shareholders. Kodak, one of the greatest trademarks in world history, went bankrupt, destroyed by computer technology. The list goes on. In 1960 no one could imagine that fate for GM. In 1980 no one could imagine that fate for Kodak.

But corporations and institutions live and die just like people and species. And the Bible, that accumulation of often counterintuitive human wisdom, teaches, "So the last shall be first and the first last."[15] Humankind at large persists and grows; people and corporations die and are replaced.

We tend to ascribe eternal properties to iconic things. We are shocked by our aging celebrities. "He (she) got so old!" If you care to be an iconic celebrity with endurance, the best career advice is to die young and leave a youthful, eternal image in the media, ever young and powerful. But even the dead icons of the past, movie sirens and heroes of the screen, are forgotten. The baton passes, and the young have their own icons who, they presume to be ageless like themselves. They believe they will never grow old, sick, or infirm and never die, crippled and feeble, in a nursing home.

So what's the point of this depressing note? It is that, contrary to our wishes and dreams, there is no forever stock just as there is no forever person. But the broad market, like the world population, like the flora and fauna of Darwin, grows and multiplies. Absent a world catastrophe—a meteor strike, a concerted nuclear exchange—it will grow, and your wealth will grow with it, slowly and inexorably, in fits and starts, the only sure bet.

---

15   Matthew 20:16.

CHAPTER 2

The Fear of Loss: Poignancy Overrewarded

We all hate to lose. Calling someone a loser qualifies as fighting words. Ever search for hours for something you lost and spend a fortune in time when you could have replaced it cheaply and easily? Ever replace it and find it later and hate yourself for replacing it? How inefficient! Ever pine for a lost love and meet him or her years later and think, "What was I pining over?" Do you know why eBay writes, "It's getting away! You're about to miss out! You missed out!"?

Because eBay is using your fear of loss to inveigle you into bidding yet again, for something you might not really need in the first place. Do you know why Costco makes items appear and disappear from the shelves? Not because they found or didn't find a good deal. Costco calls it "the treasure hunt." If you fear you might lose out on a purchase, you are more likely to buy it, whether you need it or not.

Marketers know you don't want to experience loss: neither the loss of something you possess nor the loss of something you nearly possessed. The most poignant song in the musical *South Pacific* is "This Nearly Was Mine."[16]

If you've ever come home to a burglarized home, if you've ever been mugged, you know the pain of loss. Under the Common Law of England, robbery was a felony punishable by death. In the ancient world, thieves were deprived of a hand—a barbaric punishment, but considered commensurate with the crime. How many sales

---

16 Richard Rodgers and Oscar Hammerstein, *This Nearly Was Mine* (New York: Williamson Music, Inc., 1949).

have been closed when a seasoned salesperson tells an innocent buyer: "It's the last one, and I might not be getting any more in anytime soon."

Loss is the foremost cause of major depression. Everyone has watched friends and relatives fight to save a dead romance or marriage just to avoid the pain of loss. As rock-and-roller Neil Sedaka wrote and sang, "breaking up is hard to dooo."[17] Remember Mama's advice to the brokenhearted: "Plenty of fish in the sea." Mama said it because it is not intuitive. There's even a dating site called Plenty of Fish. And who isn't moved when Judy Garland sings "The Man That Got Away" in *A Star is Born*?[18] Remember the bad breaker-upper from *Seinfeld*, the person who so hates the breakup that he must destroy the other person to get over her.[19] Think of all the great movies that turn on loss:

Citizen Kane[20] turns on lost mother-love and a futile reparative quest for self-worth through power and materialism.

Casablanca turns on lost romantic love, lost morals, and lost resolve.

Gone with the Wind[21] is just loss, loss, and more loss—lost family, lost world, lost child, lost romance, and lost marriage.

I first saw *Gone with the Wind* as a teenager traveling in Europe. On a rainy day, I ducked into a Brussels movie theater and witnessed an equivalent spectacle off-screen—a row of Belgian women wailing and crying their eyes out. Twice invaded in a generation, Belgians could identify with the sorrows and losses of war, even thousands of miles away, a hundred years ago, in a different culture, and in a foreign language. The pain of loss is universal.

---

17 Neil Sedaka and Howard Greenfield, *Breaking Up Is Hard to Do* (New York: Sony/ATV Music Publishing, 1962).

18 *A Star is Born*, Dir. George Cukor, Warner Brothers, 1954, Film; Harold Arlen and Ira Gershwin, *The Man That Got Away* (New York: Alfred Publishing Company, 1953).

19 "The Andrea Doria," *Seinfeld*, Castle Rock Entertainment, December 19, 1996, Television.

20 *Citizen Kane*, Dir. Orson Welles, RKO Radio Pictures, 1941, Film.

21 *Gone with the Wind*, Dir. Victor Fleming, Selznick International Pictures, Metro-Goldwyn-Mayer, 1939, Film.

I worked my way through law school as a bellhop. On my first day, a seasoned old salt of a bell captain warned me: "You'll remember the guests that stiff you better than the ones who tip you well." Was that ever true.

Every apartment building, town, or city has its share of hoarders. Those hoarders' homes are filled with accumulated junk they cannot discard. No one can even enter these fire-hazard, health-hazard abodes. What motivates hoarders is the fear of loss. They cannot part with anything, overwhelmed by the anticipated loss. When they are involuntarily forced to clean up and out by relatives, landlords, or authorities, they often feel better for it. But they cannot anticipate that. The pain of loss is too great.

Evolutionary psychologists have proven experimentally that loss hurts at least twice, perhaps three times as much as gain feels good. So we are wired to overreact to losses. Why? Probably it is in our animal nature to hold on to what we have. In a feral world, it might save our lives. Charlie Munger likes to talk about the Munger dog: the sweetest dog never bites anyone…unless you try to take food from its mouth. Early life lesson: never tease a dog, any dog. That dog lives in all of us, and it can undermine your ability to get rich.

How? The single biggest mistake most investors make is to sell into a collapsing market. Why is it a mistake? Because the market always comes back. Always. Even if it takes a while. So why do people sell? Because their deepest, oldest, and most powerful emotions, the same ones that make us fight to survive, tell us to avoid loss and to sell and preserve whatever we can in a time of crisis. This emotion does not exempt brilliant people—I have known two full professors who fell prey to it, one a professor of finance. Later, when the market recovers, these sellers learn that the buyers on the other side of that trade, who kept their heads, knew better. As the fiendish Mr. Potter does in *It's a Wonderful Life*, they picked up some bargains in a crashing market. And those who shop for bargains in crashes do very well. In the 2008 banking crisis, Berkshire Hathaway bought Wells Fargo at eight dollars a share. At this writing it sells for over fifty-one dollars a share.

Warren Buffett famously teaches, "Be fearful when others are greedy and greedy when others are fearful."[22] Buy low, and sell high. That's a simple but powerful maxim because driven by the fear of loss, most people will intuitively do the precise opposite. We want to buy popular things with the trendy, jubilant crowd. The most famous cautionary tale about this practice is the story of the Nifty Fifty. Briefly, it was the sorry idea to buy the best stocks regardless of cost because they were the best. It led many investors to overpay and lose money when the market awakened to the mispricing. Far better to buy unpopular but sound stocks when the thought makes you want to die. But most people cannot do that. A reasonable compromise can be to buy solid dividend-bearing stocks and reinvest the dividends—free of brokerage fees—in the underlying stock, in fair weather or foul, keeping your emotions out of play. Research has shown this to be an effective wealth-builder and avoids the human tendency to buy high and sell low.

Our perceptions of loss can be just as skewed when we lose hugely but slowly, over time. Inflation causes terrible losses to savers who are not investors, even if the central banks keep the inflation rate to the imperceptible 2 percent. Just as we misperceive the effects of compounding on our gains (discussed in chapter 6), we underappreciate the compounding of our losses.

Here is a simple thought experiment:

In 1980 your eccentric Uncle Horace leaves you his house and the legend of a million dollars hidden within. Despite your grief, you move in promptly upon his demise and search for the million high and low, but you never find it. You are now convinced it was Uncle Horace's little joke upon his heir. In 2010 your beloved wife insists on creating a great room out of the former living room, dining room, and kitchen. Lo and behold, when the wall between the kitchen and the living room is demolished, a dusty leather suitcase bearing Horace's initials is discovered with a million dollars cash within. Hallelujah! Great luck! Now you can pay for the renovation with

---

22 www.investopedia.com/articles/investing/012116/warren-buffett-be-fearful-when-others-are-greedy.asp?ad=dirN&qo=investopediaSiteSearch&qsrc=0&o=40186 (accessed September 17, 2017).

ease and have a small fortune to spare. But what is the actuarial reality? You have sustained a nearly $2 million loss! That money was worth the equivalent of $2.8 million in 1980, and inflation has been eating it away inside that wall as certain as termites. Would that Horace had been a goldbug and hid gold in that suitcase. You would be *really* wealthy now! But there will be no tears over the lost millions unless an accountant breaks the spell with the bad news. Our minds just don't work that way.

Likewise, I never tally or think about the money I have lost investing in Ford and GM, Bethlehem Steel and Citibank, the fallen or dwarfed stars of past decades. I am shielded by denial, avoidance, and all the other emotional defenses that rush to protect my investing ego and the thought that all that money would have done far better in a plain vanilla Vanguard account!

Nature protects us against some types of losses but not others. We are not wired to think we can defeat a lion or a bear or a professional boxer. Common sense and the survival instinct predominate. Very beautiful women rightly complain that most men will not approach them for dates, fearing humiliation in rejection and loss of face.

People will not avoid loss if the loss is deferred with credit-card debt, long-term loans, or pay-as-you-go schemes. My kind and generous office manager has taught a few patients who were novice retailers how to install a credit-card system. Their businesses promptly went to profit despite the pinch of the credit-card company's fees.

People who cannot or will not part with (or lose) hard cash do not mind handing over a credit card. The bill won't arrive for weeks, and then you might not quickly open it, or you could hide it from a spouse. The credit-card companies don't mind— there are more fees and penalties down the road.

Casinos replace your cash with chips. The gambling public doesn't perceive chips as cash. So losers are anesthetized as the casino performs a walletectomy. A newly minted basement-dweller can then recover his or her senses in that damp dungeon that is now home.

We can also be anesthetized against loss by the crowd phenomenon—casinos are not lonely places!

We can also benumb ourselves through training or with youthful bravado or naiveté. The most horrifying war documentary you will never see broadcast is John Huston's *The Battle of San Pietro*.[23] John Huston was a brave man. He loved riding in the steeplechase, the most dangerous horse competition by far. Huston left Hollywood during World War II and, at the War Department's request, filmed a platoon of American GIs attempting to take a hill in Italy, protected by seasoned German troops who were dug in and fortified. In the vivid 35mm footage, we meet our troops: young, handsome, and brave, bracing for combat, confident and earnest, moving forward.

Then the horrifying result: the same men on stretchers, wounded, dead, and maimed. It is riveting and soul wrenching. Not surprisingly, the film had limited release, as it was far too painful for general consumption in wartime or anytime.

Why do I put the reader through the pain of learning about *San Pietro*? To realize we can be trained to face loss, even loss of life and limb, with nobility and equanimity. The BBC once asked Charlie Munger what he thought about the then-breathtaking 50 percent drop in the market value of Berkshire Hathaway.[24] Most of his money and reputation are at Berkshire. He summarily dismissed the supposed crisis on camera with perfect aplomb. He was speaking the truth. It had happened three times. Charlie Munger did not care. He had the same response as a highly trained and experienced surgeon incising yet another abdomen—a seasoned professional facing risks with level-headed determination.

If you are going to invest, you must adopt this very same attitude to loss. The great Jack Bogle, who we will meet later in this book, advises investors in Vanguard to never look at their accounts, blindly invest until they retire, and then open the latest statement with a cardiologist nearby in case they faint at the shock of the enormity of their holdings.[25]

---

23   *The Battle of San Pietro*, Dir. John Huston, United States War Department, 1945, Film.

24   https://www.youtube.com/watch?v=3XIBrohrIUc (accessed September 17, 2017).

25   time.com/money/3983178/vanguard-founder-jack-bogle-retirement-advice/(accessed September 17, 2017).

Ben Graham, the Columbia professor who was Warren Buffett's chief mentor in youth, developed the very valuable concept of *Mr. Market*. The term sounds simple and childlike, and it is. But it is very instructive. Mr. Market is a strange little fellow who represents the stock market. The real stock exchanges are, of course, formidable and intimidating, stately buildings, like courthouses and congresses, meant to give them weight and prestige. The image of Mr. Market cuts them down to very human proportions—even more so because Mr. Market has decided mood swings. His mood rises and falls. It is unpredictable and whimsical at times; at other times it is in clear reaction to political, social, and economic events. When Mr. Market's mood is elevated and he sees only blue skies overhead, he offers stocks at inflated prices; when his mood is low, he loses hope and faith and desperately sells everything off cheaply. Real-life salespeople give up when a prospect turns them down repeatedly. Not Mr. Market. He comes back to try to sell to you again and again, whether you buy or not. When his mood settles, his prices eventually fall or rise to realistic and efficient estimates of the true worth of his stocks.

As Charlie Munger repeatedly asks, "How could it be otherwise?" The actual stock market is not in those awesome buildings on Wall Street. The stock market is a crowd. Crowds are unruly, labile, and easily susceptible to becoming cruel mobs or exultant celebrants. So why shouldn't prices of stocks go up and down if a crowd is in charge of the prices? What Warren Buffett and Charlie Munger realize, and what you must if you are to be a sober investor, is that stocks represent a part ownership of a business. If the business is sound, the value of that stock persists regardless of what the crowd says it's worth. Your parents warned you about hanging out with the wrong crowd for good reason. It can skew your judgment and lead you to a bad end.

To put a softer edge on it, follow Warren Buffett's advice: "The market is there to serve you, not to inform you."[26] Get your education by learning to understand the market rather than by watching its often random fluctuations.

---

26 www.businessdictionary.com/article/896/investing-lessons-of-warren-buffett/(accessed September 17, 2017).

CHAPTER 3

Hidden Inflation: The Incredible Shrinking Dollar

When I was a kid in the 1950s, after school my friends and I liked to patrol the local streets, eyes peeled for discarded returnable soda bottles. We got a penny for the little bottles and two cents for the quarts. If we gathered enough and brought them to Bohack's Supermarket, we could collect ten pennies to make a dime and buy a "Spaldeen" rubber ball—really a Spalding—and play games in the street.

Forty years later, I observed scattered pennies on my then eight-year-old daughter's bedroom floor and asked her why she didn't pick them up. "Dad, they're not worth anything."

My first thought was that I have spoiled my child. My second thought, the correct one, was that this eight-year-old was quite accurate. Those pennies weren't worth anything anymore. The dollar I once knew is not worth a dime. The dime I knew isn't worth a penny. The penny I knew is…close to worthless. That's inflation.

When I was eight, if my mother was not at home at lunchtime, I sometimes went for lunch at the neighborhood deli: two Hebrew National franks with mustard and sauerkraut, a square factory-made knish, a Dr. Brown's cherry soda, and a nickel change from a dollar for candy. That meal today would cost closer to twenty dollars if you could find a decent deli. But as a physician, I have to warn you against that delicious meal: all carbs, cholesterol, and fat. But, boy, it tasted good; in my mind's mouth, I taste it still.

That's food nostalgia and price nostalgia. Food nostalgia is fine: it's warm, and it's fuzzy with mouthfeel to boot. Price nostalgia is more problematic because we inevitably wish we had those prices back and our dollars had real buying power again. But we don't dare wish for that. Ask any economist: that would be deflationary, which would mean there was no demand for goods and services, a sure sign recession or depression was just down the road or already here!

The consensus among modern economists is that a low rate of inflation—about 2 percent—is the healthiest condition for the long-term growth of a modern economy.

Compounded over decades, 2 percent inflation produces the enormous price increases we can see in my nostalgic example. The further consensus is that inflation is not an inherent evil unless it is runaway inflation, which destroys economies and nations and was likely a contributing cause of World War II.

Bottom line: Inflation is a fact of life in modern economies under fiat currencies. We can debate about it, but we must live with it. What we need not debate is whether we have had more prosperity under fiat currencies than under the gold standard. We are far more prosperous now. Anyway, we're not going back to the gold standard (see chapter 4). So how do we deal with inflation?

First, we look at the upside. As I already discussed, controlled inflation and prosperity seem to correlate in our post–world war economies. Moreover, inflation is a boon to debtors who get to pay back their loans in ever-inflating dollars. That means the interest on the mortgage you take out to buy your home, which is deductible from income tax, and the principle you borrowed will be repaid with cheaper dollars. That is savings to you.

Less appealing is the fact that any money you hold in cash—and you must have some money in cash for daily expenses, emergencies, investing, and sheer peace of mind—is slowly diminishing in value each and every day, because ordinary bank deposits no longer earn any interest. That does not appear to be changing any time soon.

But the most important aspect of inflation you must understand is that you can no longer save your way to prosperity. If you simply save money, you are losing that savings to inflation. (See the tale of Uncle Horace's bequest in chapter 2.) You might not intuit that fact because, as Glenn Ford says in the opening of *Gilda*,[27] "A dollar is a dollar in any language." That's true, in 1946 and today. But a dollar is not the same dollar at any time—its value is changeable and ultimately eroding.

So how do you deal with that? You outrun inflation by investing in assets, assets that retain or, better yet, increase their value amid ups and downs over time. With some exceptions due to blight—urban, suburban, and rural—houses do that. The elegant Spanish-style house Fred MacMurray snickers about at the opening of the 1944 classic film noir *Double Indemnity*,[28] where his fate is soon to be sealed, "must have cost somebody thirty thousand bucks if they ever finished paying for it." Few homes anywhere in the United States sell for $30,000 today, and that particular one, which is still standing, unchanged, today, is listed at $2.2 million by Redfin, an online real-estate site.

This book is not about real-estate investing. It is about the sort of investing that. anyone can do from an armchair, what Charlie Munger calls "sit on your ass investing."[29] The stock market. As Charlie Munger wisely pointed out in a recent talk with fans,[30] real-estate investment requires intimate knowledge of the business, the properties, the locale, and the current state of the market, and savvy real-estate market insiders already have that knowledge. Moreover, those insiders usually have the best deals already sewn up. Finally, this type of investing is labor intensive; it's a lot of work to buy, sell, and maintain real property.

The stock market is open to everyone every weekday. Talk about a dollar and a dream! The stock market, if approached wisely, is the best place for anyone to outrun inflation and grow his or her wealth despite the eroding value of the dollar. And

---

27 *Gilda*, Dir. Charles Vidor, Columbia Pictures, 1946, Film.

28 *Double Indemnity*, Dir. Billy Wilder, Paramount Pictures, 1944, Film.

29 www.talkativeman.com/sit-on-your-ass-investing-charlie-munger/(accessed   September   17, 2017).

30 https://www.youtube.com/watch?v=RpzrHPYWojY (accessed September 17, 2017).

you can operate from anywhere by smartphone or Internet. The Dow Jones Industrial Average, the longest-standing market index of US stocks, has returned roughly 7 percent since Fred MacMurray entered that Spanish mansion in 1944, more than 11 percent if you chart earnings with reinvested dividends. If instead of buying that house for $30,000 in 1944, you invested at a 7 percent return, that $30,000 would have grown to more than $4 million today. With dividends reinvested, it would become more than $60 million—that is, exclusive of taxes on dividends. Of course, you can live in a house. You can't live in the stock market. But you have to maintain a house, and that costs money. Costs of maintaining a brokerage or retirement account are nominal today, especially if you wisely trade rarely and only when the odds are with you, which we will get to later in the book.

PART II

Growing Your Money

CHAPTER 4

Fool's Gold and Golden Parachutes

Our fiat currencies—our dollars and euros—are created by the central banks. They are not backed by precious metals as they once were but by the faith and credit of the central banks and the governments. So unlike gold or money backed by gold, the money supply can be regulated, expanded, or contracted to stimulate the economy or control the inevitable inflation of paper currency. Central banks try to keep that inflation rate at 2 percent. Why 2 percent? Because experience teaches that the general population can accept a 2 percent inflation rate without experiencing distress.

High inflation weakens an economy, and hyperinflation destroys nations. But the public's time horizon is short—a 2 percent loss in the value of paper money per year is hardly noticeable. "There is no inflation" sounds roughly right. Because inflation compounds slowly and almost invisibly, only Grandpa recalls the five-cent slice of pizza or five-cent subway ride that now costs three dollars. Note that movie writers cleverly keep home prices and salaries out of their screenplays, lest latter-day viewers guffaw as actors gasp over a $25,000 home or a $15,000 annual salary. The vaunted "millionaires" of the 1920s and 1930s have been replaced by the billionaires of the new millennium. So many modern suburban homeowners are now de facto "millionaires" through inflation that the term has lost its cachet.

So how do you hedge against inflation? How do you keep the value of your money? Some people insist that gold is the answer. Wall Street derisively calls them gold-bugs because the idea is a little "buggy" after you sort it out. It is essentially true that gold retains its value and paper money does not, at least not since it ceased to be redeemable for gold. An ounce of gold in 1951, when I was born, was worth forty dollars.

Today, it is worth $1,250. If you bought gold in 1951, would you have beaten inflation? Yes. According to the US Inflation Calculator[31] online, it would take $376 in today's dollars to match forty dollars' buying power in 1951. But is that the whole story? No. The most apt comparison is not gold and paper money because we know paper money is subject to inflation and hoarding cash at zero interest long term is financial disaster. The apt comparison is between gold and the stock market. Where would those forty dollars be if invested in the Dow Jones Industrial Average for the same sixty-five years? The results are shocking! Without dividends reinvested and with no deduction for fees or taxes, at the historical 7 percent, that money would be about $3,200! With dividends reinvested in a nontaxable account and with no fees, that would be roughly 10 percent compounded—about $19,570! These figures are both astronomical and counterintuitive, but they are real!

So where does that leave the argument for investing in gold? To be sure, the metal is beautiful. Gold has been associated with wealth and splendor since antiquity. It is a metaphor for wealth, power, and beauty. But the best argument for owning gold is a hedge against an apocalyptic event: nuclear war, revolution, depression, hyperinflation, plague, natural disaster, meteor strike, and so on. None of us think much about that unless we work for a think tank, move in the highest reaches of government or the military, or have become paranoid or psychotic. Machiavelli noted that no one looking at calm seas contemplates a storm.[32] Yet, as history proves, the risk is real, and we all probably live in happy denial. If you have gold in a cataclysm, you are more likely to survive. Europeans who lived through World War II can still, in living memory, tell you gold can save your life. No one can wisely criticize a choice to keep some money in gold, and God help us all if you do and eventually have the last laugh. If you keep any money in gold, keep it secure and, in Mario Puzo's mother's phrase when she heard that he received $410,000 for the paperback rights to The Godfather,[33] "Don't tell nobody."[34] Gold can be lost to intimates, employees, contractors, fiduciaries, incapacity, and death. Remember "buried treasure" once belonged to someone!

31   www.usinflationcalculator.com/ (accessed September 17, 2017).

32   Niccolo Machiavelli, The Prince (New York: Cambridge University Press, 1988).

33   Mario Puzo, The Godfather (New York: G.P. Putnam & Sons, 1969).

34   www.slate.com/articles/arts/culturebox/2003/05/the_godmother.html/(accessed   September 17, 2017).

CHAPTER 5

Luck and Probability: The Lure of the Bad Bet

The concept of luck is as old as humankind. It is as irresistible as it is irrational. We thoughtlessly wish luck upon ourselves, our families, and our friends. The worse the situation, the more we wish for good luck. No matter how much we advance in our thinking, no matter how much science, technology, and probability theory we digest, we still, intuitively, believe in luck. Runs of luck, good luck charms and talismans, lucky days, favorites of the gods, lucky dogs, and lucky devils. We believe that luck runs out and admonish others not to press their luck. We cast our fates to the wind and kick over the traces, thinking Lady Luck and Dame Fortune will protect us.

Survivors of the worst risks—war and disaster—feel very lucky indeed. We, the observers, perceive them as lucky as well. This optimism has even led to CD collections like *Songs of World War II*. Think that over. Millions bombed, burned alive, gassed, machinegunned, torn apart by shrapnel—agonizing deaths, the sheer horror of which defies the imaginations of the generations who did not live through it, and there are song collections to celebrate that war. The people who buy those CDs and listen to those songs and wax nostalgic about the war are the very people who survived it.

Churchill said there is nothing so exhilarating as to be shot at and missed.[35] So why shouldn't these people believe in luck? We are their descendants, and why shouldn't we believe in luck? The unlucky are the dead. They are not here to plead their case

---

35 https://www.brainyquote.com/quotes/quotes/w/winstonchu100445.html (accessed September 17, 2017).

that luck does not exist, only cold randomness and probability, the stuff of math and science. But it's the math and science that are actually true! Luck is an illusion.

If you believe in luck and not in randomness and probability, there are no good or bad bets, only good and bad luck. Lottery operators, casino magnates, and croupiers love people who believe in luck—they fill casino coffers. Believers in luck won't rationally evaluate the games they play and, just as rationally, refuse the bad bets.

How does the public respond to lottery winners and Vegas winners? We congratulate them on their good luck and their good fortune as they gush with pride. But what is the scientific truth behind their success? Just imagine what the most coldly rational of our TV and movie characters, Mr. Spock of *Star Trek* or Dr. Sheldon Cooper on *Big Bang Theory*, might say to these winners: "Rationally speaking, the winner had to be someone. And randomly it was you."

What a heartless putdown! To which Dr. Cooper and Mr. Spock might respond, "It is the objective truth. There is no other plausible explanation." And indeed it is so. Our System One, our common sense, loves the winners of bad bets. System Two, our book-smart brain, knows this was a random process that turned out well for one individual and took the multitudes for their money. The winner just happens to have won a bad bet. A bad lesson for that winner and for everyone else who thinks, "That could have been me."

What is a bad bet? A bad bet is a bet you are very, very likely to lose. It is the proverbial sucker's bet. Why would anyone take such a bad bet, particularly when there are good bets around, even sure bets? From a purely rational perspective, using System Two, as we should, a good bet is always better than a bad bet, and a sure bet is the best bet of all. But System One does not work that way.

People choose bad bets all the time. They buy lottery tickets and play the numbers, the horses, crap tables, roulette wheels, slots, and blackjack—bets where they risk all they bet on the off chance they might win big. Why? Behavioral psychologist

B.F. Skinner felt he had the complete answer in reinforcement theory.[36] All animals in his experiments responded best to irregular and unpredictable rewards, like those of bad bets in gambling.

Charlie Munger, Daniel Kahneman, and Amos Tversky have looked more deeply at this question and found other, more nuanced reasons as well. Kahneman and Tversky teach us the key concept of availability.[37] We tend to ignore the simple reality that we can only choose from what is available. Criminals have no problem discerning availability. When he was asked why he robbed banks, Willie Sutton shot back, "That's where the money is."[38] Bad bets are highly available, and they are in your face all the time. Lottery tickets and casinos are advertised on TV and billboards and featured on the news. The public chats them up. Good bets are not advertised, and sure bets, like stock-market index funds, are well hidden in plain sight.

Second are associations. Bad bets are vivid and exciting. Vegas, showgirls, beautiful people, celebrities, alcohol, entertainment, joy, popularity, movies, and happiness. We respond viscerally to all things associated with gambling. Movie writers, directors, and producers love to put casinos into their movies; the audience response is rapturous. Think of the slow pans of the faces of high-rolling gamblers in *Casablanca*, *Casino Royale*, *Casino*, and *Gilda*. We are bored by the mundane and the humdrum, even when it is the better bet. In his book, *What Works on Wall Street*, James O'Shaughnessy recounts how clients are thrilled with quoted returns on his stock picks until they learn how dull and unglamorous the actual stocks are and foolishly refuse to buy them.[39] I was always excited over my auto stocks—Ford, GM, and Toyota—and lost money on every one. Berkshire Hathaway's most recent big acquisition was Precision Castparts.[40] Precision

---

36 Terry J. Knapp, "Behaviorism and Public Policy: B. F. Skinner's Views on Gambling," *Behavior and Social Issues* 7, no. 2 (Fall 1997): 129–39.

37 A. Tversky and D. Kahneman, "Availability: A Heuristic for Judging Frequency and Probability," *Cognitive Psychology* 5 (1973): 207–32.

38 Robert M. Yoder, "Someday They'll Get Slick Willie," *Saturday Evening Post* 223, no. 30 (January 20, 1951).

39 James P. O'Shaughnessy, *What Works on Wall Street* (New York: McGraw-Hill Education, 2011).

40 www.wsj.com/articles/berkshire-hathaway-to-buy-precision-castparts-1439205293(accessed September 17, 2017).

Castparts makes aerospace-related gizmos you'll never see and only engineers and technicians know about. But you can be sure they are a good bet.

Third is the thrill of risk. It is very risky to take a bad bet, and we intuitively admire risk-takers. Winning at something risky is a rush. Even risk-takers who lose are admired as high rollers and are catered to, comped and flattered, at the casinos and are admired for "taking it like a man" when they lose. Winning that's a foregone conclusion—shooting fish in a barrel—is dull and even cowardly.

Several times in my practice, I have met US Army Air Force combat veterans of World War II, men who flew missions over occupied Europe and lived to tell the tale. One of them was shot down and was saved by the Resistance. I was thrilled to be in their presence, and the thrill remains to this day. Risk-takers in combat win our admiration and love. Combat soldiers in Israel have more romantic encounters than desk-bound or support troops. "You gotta be a football hero to get the love of a beautiful girl," goes the 1933 hit song.[41]

Our entertainments are filled with good-looking people taking huge risks and lucking out. No matter what hell the screenwriters drag them through, they are alive at the end for the next installment. That's what sells tickets and keeps eyeballs glued to the screens and asses in the seats. There is a classic 1956 sci-fi flick ineptly titled *Invasion of the Body Snatchers*.[42] Don't let that title fool you. This is an expertly crafted paranoid thriller of an alien invasion, directed by Don Siegel, who is credited for the brilliant montages in *Casablanca*. It has top-flight acting, script, and direction. *Spoiler alert.* There was one problem: the aliens won. It could not be released because it was hopelessly noncommercial. So a framing device was written and shot. Earth wins in the end, which saved the picture and Kevin McCarthy, the family physician—the hero. (I liked that.)

Our movie heroes must take breathtaking risks and survive, or we would not love them so. By contrast, the villains in the Bond films all play it safe. They have untold

---

41 Al Sherman, Buddy Fields, and Al Lewis, *You Gotta Be a Football Hero* (New York: Leo Feist, Inc., 1933).

42 *Invasion of the Body Snatchers*, Dir. Don Siegel, Allied Artists Pictures, 1956, Film.

wealth, mercenary armies, flunkies, and stooges galore. Bond has guts, brains, strength, charm, and, most of all, luck. He is the favorite of the gods and—at least in the books and films—always wins. And we identify with movie heroes. Every guy walks a little taller leaving a Bond picture. When he wins, we win. Who roots for Goldfinger?[43] Not even Mrs. Goldfinger, divorced and angry, wherever she is. You can be sure Goldfinger's kids hate him and await his death as eagerly as Bond does.

Gambling plays upon another misapprehension identified by Kahneman and Tversky—survivorship bias. It is a cousin of availability. We only see the winners, the survivors. The losers are MIA. There are no TV features on lottery losers, no news stories about broke suckers at casinos, no magazine features on the guys who quit their day jobs to play the options markets and are crapped out. But psychiatrists see the devastated families living in basement apartments, the disgusted spouses who will never again trust the persons with whom they have spent their lives and raised their children, and the attempted and completed suicides.

There are no do-overs in lotteries, casinos, or the financial markets. No refunds for discontented players. Just maybe a referral to Gamblers Anonymous or a mental-health clinic.

So let's premedicate you with this System Two book-smart knowledge: it is not mathematically likely that any person will consistently win taking bad bets. It is never a reasonable way to try to get rich. Yet I hear it in my office all the time: "If I ever win the lottery! Maybe I'll win the lottery!" The best explanation I have ever heard for the phenomenal success of state lotteries is this—it is an ignorance tax. The only tax you don't have to pay!

Charlie Munger says he wants to shoot fish in a barrel after the water has been drained out.[44] He waits patiently, years if necessary, for the surest bet he can find and then bets heavily. The only smart gamble is gambling when the odds are with you, even if it is not as much fun.

---

43 *Goldfinger*, Dir. Guy Hamilton, United Artists, 1964, Film.
44 https://twitter.com/farnamstreet/status/581826731503427584 (accessed September 17, 2017).

There is a marvelous old *Twilight Zone* episode out of the first season called "A Nice Place to Visit."[45] *Spoiler alert!* Small-time gambler and hood, Henry Valentine, is shot to death in a failed robbery and awakens in a magical, immaculate world where a jovial Sebastian Cabot, whom we presume is an angel, assures that his every wish is granted, every gamble won, and every win assured. He accumulates gambling wins and romantic conquests, until, bored and angry, he protests that this is no heaven for him. And, of course, it's not heaven at all; it's the other place.

That's because for Valentine it was never the win that drew him. It was the thrill of the risk. Without risk his games yield no pleasure. So as Rod Serling snickers his conclusory admonishments, we absorb the message: there is a little Henry Valentine in all of us, seeking the thrill of the risk of gambling rather than the reasonable returns of playing it safe.

---

45 "A Nice Place to Visit," *The Twilight Zone*, Cayuga Productions, April 15, 1960, Television.

CHAPTER 6

The Power of the Force: Compounding

I n *Star Wars: A New Hope*, Obi-Wan Kenobi introduces Luke Skywalker to the Force: "An energy field created by all living things. It surrounds us, penetrates us, and binds the galaxy together." It may surprise you to learn there really is a force in nature as powerful as the Force in *Star Wars*. It is no fantasy. Like the *Star Wars* Force, it has infinite and unstoppable power. Like the *Star Wars* Force, it has a light and a dark side. The light side enriches and ennobles those who embrace it. Pity the poor souls who, like Darth Vader, are seduced by the dark side of this real-life force.

The force is called "compound interest." It is not included in the toolkit of common sense. It requires book smarts to understand. If you glean but a single idea from this book, it should be this quote attributed to Albert Einstein, the real-life model for Yoda[46] in *Star Wars*: "Compound interest is the most powerful force in the Universe. The Eighth Wonder of the World. He who understands it, earns it. He who doesn't, pays it."[47]

Compound interest is one idea from Einstein that is comparatively easy to understand. The other is the thought experiment that we will meet again later in this chapter.

---

46   mentalfloss.com/article/71795/how-einstein-influcenced-yoda-look (accessed September 17, 2017).

47   www.quotesonfinance.com/quote/79/Albert-Einstein-Compound-Interest (accessed September 17, 2017).

Let's begin with basics. There is simple interest. You lend $100.00—that's your principal—at 5 percent interest. The first year you receive $5.00 interest back on your principal, and your account balance is now $105.00. The second year you get another fiver, and your account balance is $110.00. Each year, another $5.00. Quite simple, and it is called "simple interest." Because there is no interest on the interest, only on the principal. Well, who cares about interest on interest? It must be chump change. That is true, at first. But read on.

Compound interest is simple interest plus the interest on the simple interest, compounded once, twice, or four times a year. I'll keep it simple and do a calculation for once per year. So lending $100.00 at compound interest yields the same $105.00 in year one.

But year two is not $110.00. It is $110.25 with a mere $0.25 in interest on the $5.00 you received as simple interest. Chump change for sure. But in ten years' time when simple interest has yielded $150.00, compound interest has grown to $162.89. In twenty years when simple has yielded $200.00, compound interest has grown to $265.33. In fifty years simple interest yields $350.00, but compound interest now displays the power of the force: $1,146.74. Do you begin to get the point? If you have a higher interest rate, compound interest grows bigger and faster. At 10 percent, the rough historical return of the S&P 500, the thirty-year figure is $1,744.94 and the fifty-year figure is $11,739.09. With a long enough time frame, more frequent compounding, and regular contributions to principal, in the words of Leo Bloom in *The Producers*,[48] "A man could make a fortune!" Except unlike Max and Leo in *The Producers*, it's perfectly legal and risk free, involves no effort, and harms no one. It's what Charlie Munger likes to call "sit on your ass investing."[49]

Let's take a real-life example. A twenty-five-year-old earns $50,000 per year and vows to save $5,000 per year in a tax-deferred retirement account over a fortyyear working life. The person seeks only a 5 percent return through very conservative investing—for example, preferred shares of stable corporations. No

---

48   *The Producers*, Dir. Mel Brooks, Embassy Pictures, 1967, Film.
49   www.talkativeman.com/sit-on-your-ass-investing-charlie-munger/(accessed September 17, 2017).

growth, just reinvested dividends. The future value of the investments is $674,164 at retirement. Make that return rate 10 percent, the rough historical return of the S&P 500, and it grows to $2,660,555. Amp up the savings with anticipated raises and perks to $10,000 per year: $5,321,110. Work to age seventy-five, and it balloons to $13,976,902. You can use one of the online compound-interest calculators and prove it to yourself. That's how I was taught organic chemistry by the late Professor Wolff at Columbia University: do it yourself, and prove it to yourself.

Perhaps the best illustration of the counterintuitive nature of compound interest is the following trick question. Which would you rather have: one million dollars right now or a penny doubled every day for a month? Common sense tells you to take the million and run. But put on your thinking cap and run it through the calculator for thirty or thirty-one days of the month:

Day	Amount
1	$0.01
2	$0.02
3	$0.04
4	$0.08
5	$0.16
6	$0.32
7	$0.64
8	$1.28
9	$2.56
10	$5.12
11	$10.24
12	$20.48
13	$40.96
14	$81.92
15	$163.84
16	$327.68
17	$655.36
18	$1,310.72

19	$2,621.44
20	$5,242.88
21	$10,485.76
22	$20,971.52
23	$41.943.04
24	$83,886.08
25	$167,772.16
26	$335,544.32
27	$671,088.64
28	$1,342,177.28
29	$2,684,354.56
30	$5,368,709.12
31	$10,737,418.24

Over five or ten times as much as the million dollars, depending upon whether it's a thirty-day or a thirty-one-day month! No chump change here. With a long enough runway, you take off for the wild blue yonder.

That's the force of compound interest!

You can see that compound interest has three important characteristics:

1. It is not part of the commonsense toolkit, and it is not intuitive.
2. It grows slowly but inevitably, faster and bigger with a higher rate or frequency and a longer term.
3. It flies into orbit at the end of a long, slow climb.

Applying this to daily life, you can draw three important conclusions:

1. If I compound money all my life in untaxed retirement accounts, I will grow rich as I mature.
2. If I spend my money now instead of compounding it, I will destroy my future wealth.
3. If I borrow money at interest, I might never be able to pay it off, because the compound interest on the debt will grow and keep me poor all my life.

Yes, number three is a killer! Debt at interest is the dark side of the force of compounding. Going to the dark side of compound interest is buying on credit, instead of waiting and saving for what you want or not buying at all. Remember how the thrill of gambling winnings and found money was revealed to be an addictive and dangerous drug in chapter 1. Similarly, the excitement of buying on credit can be addictive and thrilling in much the same way. All addictions corrupt and destroy. The dark side of the compounding force can seduce and destroy you and your family. That's why Warren Buffett shuns debt. It has ruined many of his fellow financial titans and many a workaday neighbor as well.

The mass public does not understand the force of compound interest. Common sense does not include the force of compound interest. But credit-card companies, loan companies, brokers, and money managers understand the force of compound interest very well. More importantly, they understand that the public does not. That is why your junk mail is filled with solicitations for credit cards, even in the names of your beloved dead relatives, previous owners and tenants, your dogs, and your cats. Credit cards bear high interest rates and compound relentlessly with late fees and penalties galore. They are money machines for the credit-card companies, who are the loan sharks of our age even as they pretend to be our benefactors and friends. Brokers and money managers who take a 1 percent or 2 percent share of your account per year know full well how it will diminish your future wealth and what it will do for their present-day income and their compounded future wealth.

Charlie Munger recommends getting rich slowly.[50] Why? Because windfall money often destroys people. Read about lottery winners. The stories are online. They are often bankrupt in a year or two: divorced, unemployed, swindled, and depressed. Found money corrupts because it was never earned. We value only what we earn. If you earn money and compound it slowly over a lifetime, not only will you have independence and comfort in old age and the ability to improve the course of your children's lives, but you will also have pride in your accomplishment, in what you have built.

What's the other reason Charlie Munger recommends getting rich slowly? It's a safer bet! If you invest and compound over a lifetime, you are almost certain to get rich. Absent disaster—atomic war, meteor strike, famine, long-term depression, and chaos—it is a near-mathematical certainty.

Let's use a cinematic example everyone knows and loves: Marilyn Monroe. Despite a tormented life and horrible death, she remains a beloved, perhaps the most beloved, star of the silver screen. In two of her most famous films, *Gentlemen Prefer Blondes*[51] and *Some Like It Hot*,[52] she portrays, for better or worse, a gold digger—a

---

50   http://www.forbes.com/sites/phildemuth/2015/04/20/charlie-munger-2015-daily-journal-an-nual-meeting-part-3/#3150a37972dd (accessed September 17, 2017).

51   *Gentlemen Prefer Blondes*, Dir. Howard Hawks, 20th Century Fox, 1953, Film.

52   *Some Like It Hot*, Dir. Billy Wilder, Mirisch Company, 1959, Film.

beautiful young woman who seeks a wealthy husband. We do not disdain her for it. As with anyone beloved, we celebrate her virtues and ignore her faults. In any case, who wouldn't be blessed to be in the company of Marilyn Monroe?

What is the single most important thing Marilyn, as Lorelei Lee and Sugar Kane, discovers in the course of the arc of each film?

Rich men are usually very old!

Yes, their wealth has been built over a lifetime of careful accumulation and compounding. And in each film she disdains the older man in favor of the young scion of the family (one real, one a pretender, Tony Curtis), so she can enjoy young love and old money at the same time. (*Spoiler alert:* When Tony turns out to be a phony millionaire, she still loves him. No gold digger after all.)

But the force of compound interest is not limited to finance. It is a force in all of life, in the expansion of populations, and in the wealth of nations. Trust compounds. Friendship compounds. Faith compounds. Honor compounds. Love compounds. It results in what Charlie Munger likes to call "a web of deserved trust." It is a force in the building of a business or a law, medical, or accounting practice. It can be a source of great joy, as Charlie Munger says, "There is huge pleasure in life to be obtained from getting deserved trust."[53] Returning again to the movies, the best cinematic example of compounded virtue and deserved trust is Frank Capra's *It's a Wonderful Life.*[54]

Let's take a good long look at the life of George Bailey, portrayed by James Stewart in the 1946 Liberty Films picture that has become the ultimate holiday evergreen—so widely viewed it needs no spoiler alerts.

In 1919 in the mythical New York town of Bedford Falls, George Bailey, a boy of twelve, risks his life to save his kid brother, Harry, from drowning. His left ear becomes

---

53   https://www.farnamstreetblog.com/2016/04/munger-operating-system/(accessed September 17, 2017).
54   *It's a Wonderful Life*, Dir. Frank Capra, Liberty Films, 1946, Film.

infected in the plunge, and he loses his hearing in that ear during the pre-antibiotic era. Then he suffers a beating—to that very left ear—to save another child's life and his pharmacist-employer's livelihood and profession. It is a fearful thing to see a drunken, grieving adult beat an innocent, bleeding child. (New viewers learn early on that this story will not be standard Hollywood fare.) When Mr. Gower, the pharmacist, realizes that George has saved both him and the child, he hugs, cries, and thanks him, and we witness one of the tenderest scenes in the history of film. George learns to employ Charlie Munger's fundamental algorithm of life: "Repeat what works!"[55] For George, what works is kindness, fairness, generosity, sacrifice, and goodness. He has been taught it by his parents, Peter and "Ma" Bailey—she is never named—who exemplify it. Careful viewers will spot an obscure sign behind the adult George Bailey's desk: "All you can take with you is that which you have given away."

Yet young George has his own dreams: he wants a million dollars, to get away from Bedford Falls, to travel, to "build modern cities," and to find adventure, excitement, and, implicitly, sexual gratification ("a couple of harems, and maybe three or four wives!"). But as a grown man, George never does anything he wants, always putting the needs of others before his own. He passes up steamy sex with Violet, the ever-available town hottie who George knows needs protection from herself. He gives up college, travel, and wealth to save his ne'er-do-well Uncle Billy, who can't run the Bailey Brothers Building & Loan Association alone after Peter Bailey dies. He sends his brother, Harry, to college and unwillingly nurtures and grows the Building & Loan to help poor townsfolk buy homes in his Bailey Park. He sacrifices for his wife, Mary, and the four children he was never sure he wanted, all of which keeps him from ever realizing his personal hopes and dreams of pleasure and wealth.

But instead of success, for all his sacrifice, George is brought to ruin by that same Uncle Billy when the befuddled near-alcoholic loses $8,000 of the company's money (over $100,000 in today's dollars) taunting old man Potter, the movie's greedy villain and Peter Bailey's nemesis, by dropping it in Potter's lap, folded in a newspaper announcing Harry Bailey's triumphant return from the war—Harry

---

55 https://www.farnamstreetblog.com/2016/12/batesian-mimicry/(accessed September 17, 2017).

Bailey, the hero that George could have been if he'd never saved his brother and become "4-F on account of his ear."

It can only get worse. George lends money to destitute Violet, who kisses him in gratitude. The lipstick smear sets off an ugly rumor of infidelity and, perhaps, a kept woman. When George begs Potter for a loan on his $15,000 life-insurance policy to replace the $8,000 Potter now holds, Potter taunts him with the rumor and calls the district attorney, telling George he is worth more dead than alive. George concludes that his only way out is to take Potter's suggestion, kill himself, and, in dying, save the Building & Loan and his soon-to-be destitute family. Even in choosing death, George is dying for others.

How can the plot now save George from an ignominious end?

Deus ex machina! A watchful heaven sends an angel, Clarence, a simple but persistent clockmaker, to apply his clockmaker's logic to save George and everyone else. The angel intervenes, most importantly by jumping into the river, obliging George to save him rather than drown himself in his planned suicide. "I jumped in the river to save you!" says Clarence. But George regrets being saved. He can see no way out of his dilemma. George wishes he were never born.

An idea is born instead. Clarence applies a simple rule of Carl Jacobi's nineteenth-century mathematics to George's world to save George and everyone else: inversion, a rule that Charlie Munger recommends to anyone with a seemingly insoluble problem. Look at the problem upside down or backward and see it afresh.[56]

Clarence also creates an Einsteinian thought experiment—given cinematic expression in a simulation that remains one of the most powerful sequences in cinema history. Clarence, with heavenly assistance, simulates for George the world as it would have been without him, the George-free decompounded world of Pottersville. "You've been given a great gift, George—the chance to see what the world would be like without you."

---

56   https://rpseawright.wordpress.com/2013/12/17/invert-always-invert/(accessed September 17, 2017).

It is the world of Bedford Falls without all the compounded love, faith, care, and trust that George has brought to it. It is a horrid, decadent, self-indulgent, amoral, inebriated, childless hell that, when compared to an $8,000 debt, a scandal, and a prison term, makes George's current troubles seem like a day at the beach. In the nightmare Georgeless world of Pottersville, unwound from George's compounded love and devotion, Harry is dead, drowned at the age of ten. Dead as well are the soldiers Harry saved in the war. Mr. Gower the druggist is the town drunk who killed a kid. Uncle Billy has been in the insane asylum since the Building & Loan went bust after George's father died. Without George to support her, Ma Bailey runs a two-bit boarding house, an embittered widow. Violet is a dime-a-dance girl or worse, rolling sailors and by inference dallying with Potter, who now owns and operates the corrupted Pottersville filled with nightclubs, strip joints, poolrooms, and bars. George's children were never born, for in the selfishness of his wish to have his life erased, he has, in effect, aborted them. The old Granville house that Mary made a home is in shambles, and poor Mary, whom we know from the beginning of the movie could love only George, is a guarded and fearful old maid (this is 1945) and the town librarian, if anyone in Pottersville reads.

The inverse thought experiment, realized so dramatically on the screen, catapults George into a new reality. His life has meaning because of what he has done for others. George experiences firsthand a mounting cascade of devastating losses (recall the discussion of loss in chapter 4), the hole left without him and its compounded consequences. George begs Clarence, "Get me back. I don't care what happens to me. Get me back to my wife and kids." And by renewed heavenly intervention, Clarence brings George back to face his fate.

But we are not done with the effects of compounding. The compounded love and devotion that George has given to others now yields the bounty that lies at the end of a compounded life well led, the seamless web of deserved trust.[57] His friends and neighbors rush to save him: he reaps what he has sown. Compounded love is repaid with love. The townspeople do not believe Potter's lies. They know George, and they know Potter. Their compounded reputations have preceded

---

57   https://www.farnamstreetblog.com/2016/04/munger-operating-system/(accessed September 17, 2017).

them. Friends, relatives, neighbors, depositors, and borrowers all pony up the $8,000 and more to save George from ruin and prison.

They don't revile him; they celebrate him. Even his wealthy childhood rival for Mary's hand, "Hee-Haw" Sam Wainwright, sends a telegram authorizing release of $25,000 (over $300,000 in today's money) to protect George from whatever trouble he is in, no questions asked. The seamless web of deserved trust borne of compounded virtue has saved our George.

We exit the movie confirmed in what we thought we knew but were never quite sure of—that virtue and goodness triumph and that a just and loving God watches over us all. The film is based upon a short story by Philip Van Doren Stern that could not find a publisher and so was sent as a Christmas card to Stern's friends and relatives and entitled—what else?—"The Greatest Gift."

But for our purposes it is ever important to remember, it is not divine intervention that saves George and Bedford Falls. Clarence is only a messenger, a Diogenes who holds up a lamp for George and the viewer to behold the compounded virtue of a life well led. Alternately, we see compounded sin and folly when, as Edmund Burke said, "good men do nothing" and "evil triumph[s]."[58]

Summing up, what have we learned in this chapter?

1. Compound interest is the true power of the force.
2. Everything compounds: investments, goodness, and virtue as well as debt, sin, and folly.
3. The light side can let you grow virtuous and rich, and the dark side can drive you to become addicted, selfish, and poor.
4. Barring tragedy, anyone can engage the light side, grow rich, and lead a wonderful life.

---

58   https://www.brainyquote.com/quotes/quotes/e/edmundburk377528.html(accessed September 17, 2017).

PART III

Keeping Your Money

CHAPTER 7

Never Be a Patsy

To get rich over a lifetime, you must recognize that there are people in the financial world who would gladly take for themselves a goodly portion of the money that would otherwise make you rich. That is a nasty thought, not socially acceptable, and for that reason tends to fly under the radar. It comes under the heading of "no one ever tells you." So I am going to.

The first concept to understand, again from Charlie Munger, is the power of incentives.[59] Incentives are both hidden and underappreciated, but they actually control much of human behavior. People will do what they are paid to do. It gives a whole new meaning to the maxim, "You get what you pay for." Think along these lines: you get what you reward. While some of us are charitable by nature or because of religion, patriotism, or professionalism, most people are dollar driven, even though they may not know it. Charlie Munger likes to tell the story of Federal Express, a company that could not get their workers to work quickly enough to accomplish the promised next-day delivery, until they were paid exclusively to get the job done, not by the shift or the hour. Incentives made the difference.

Back before managed care, when health-insurance companies allowed $1,000 for mental-health benefits to every subscriber, they found that psychiatrists and psychologists treated their patients until the benefit ran out, never more or less than the $1,000. Once a patient came in for the first visit, they continued until the $1,000 was fully paid out. Then the treatment ended. It was similar with chiropractors and physical therapists. Psychiatrists, psychologists, physical therapists, and chiropractors

---

59 Munger, "The Psychology of Human Misjudgment."

were the first victims of managed care because so much of the care they provided was apparently incentive driven. Yet all those practitioners would argue that they were merely doing their jobs and helping the patients.

They probably were. But the parameters of care were still set by the incentives.

You might say that these therapies are rife with fraud anyway. But the same incentive-driven behavior can be true of health practitioners who would appear to obey purely objective standards with measurable outcomes—surgeons. Charlie Munger has two stories of surgeons, a general surgeon who unnecessarily removed gallbladders and cardiac surgeons who performed unneeded open-heart surgery. They amassed fortunes for themselves and their hospitals. As Charlie Munger notes, nobody survives surgery better than the patient who does not need it. The surgeons never believed they were doing anything wrong, even after the belated investigations that terminated their privileges. Back in the days when cataract extractions were very well compensated, they were referred to among the eye surgeons euphemistically in private as Cadillacs. Cataract extractions have been performed on patients with advanced dementia where visual improvement would hardly be perceived or appreciated, but in the words of Chico Marx, "We charge just the same."[60]

Stock brokers and money managers are incentivized by fees for managing and servicing your accounts. If your money simply sits in an index fund compounding year after year, they earn nothing from you. If you buy and sell individual stocks or mutual funds, they collect fees. If they sell you an investment product, a managed fund, or an annuity, they earn fees from the organization whose product they are selling. Under traditional law, the broker is not a fiduciary. That is, he or she does not have a legal duty to act exclusively on your behalf and not selfdeal. Accordingly, he or she is not prohibited from promoting or selling a product that may not be optimal for you or any client. If it is in your best interest to invest in an index fund or Berkshire Hathaway and leave that investment there, unmolested, to grow and compound for forty years, rather than buy and sell individual stocks with little to show for it in the long run, the financial professional has no duty to tell you that. There is no duty to advise you not to

---

60 *Animal Crackers*, Dir. Victor Heerman, Paramount Pictures, 1930, Film.

buy and sell frequently, which typically increases his or her income and reduces your account balance. That last fact, that frequent trading leads to losses, was first observed in 1688 by Joseph de la Vega in his classic *Confusion de confusiones*, when he described the Amsterdam Stock Exchange of that era. Yet it is still news to many brokers and more of their customers. News they may never receive!

Many years ago, I told one broker I wanted to buy Berkshire Hathaway. He had a simple response: one day Warren Buffett and Charlie Munger would be dead, and where would I be then? The broker would not criticize Berkshire Hathaway. Their track record was breathtaking, defying the odds and the accepted science of the efficient market hypothesis. So all he could tell me was what most five-year-olds have sadly learned: everybody dies. The broker knew Berkshire Hathaway shareholders rarely sell. If they are smart enough to buy Berkshire Hathaway, they are likely smart enough to buy and hold. As I noted above, brokers make no money on your holdings, per se, unless they get a percentage of the account as a fee for managing it. Not a deal you want to take if you are going to buy and hold an index fund or Berkshire Hathaway and pay a lifetime of unearned fees. Few money managers can outperform an index fund or Berkshire Hathaway, but they will charge you for trying. And who would pay a fee to an account manager for an account that sits and grows without sales or purchases?

Am I saying that the finance industry at large is a con or a scam? By no means. But just like the big city or the Internet, the industry is a dangerous place where many cons and scams can operate. So let's step back. Just what is a con? In police parlance, it is an operation in which an organization or an individual gains the confidence of innocents, of "patsies," and proceeds to separate them from their money. Some are patently illegal, like the well-known Three-card Monte game once rife on the streets of New York City. But others are subtle and stay on the right side of the law, at least in principle.

The numbers racket is a con. A lottery is a con. Even a state lottery is a con, though it is regulated and the moneys go to state coffers. A casino is a con. All of them try to assure you that you can win when you are much more likely to lose. A con artist cons you by playing to your Kahneman and Tversky System One.

For this discussion let's make it very plain—your dog brain! Because you see others winning in the ads or at the casino or in the neighborhood, your dog brain anticipates that you'll win too. Dogs can't run odds. Dogs can't do math. Dogs just see other dogs getting treats and want one. So at a casino, a lotto concession, or a racetrack, you get excited like any dog and play like any dog, not realizing you are being relieved of your hard-earned money in the process. You are a patsy. You never want to be anybody's patsy. The best book you will ever read about not being a patsy is Robert Cialdini's *Influence: The Psychology of Persuasion*.[61] Cialdini is an academic psychologist who hit the bestseller list unmasking cons in everyday life. Great read!

Let's look at other cons—casinos. Casinos are always plush, with all the trappings and assurances of wealth, stability, and credibility. No bum's rush here. Just lush surroundings, good food, free liquor to disinhibit you, happy people, some winning, others happy for the winners, entertainment, and an occasional celebrity (a "top dog"). These trappings and assurances soothe and turn off System Two, your book smarts. Like the turkey who believes the farmer is a benevolent source of food and shelter, you are being led to the joys of Thanksgiving Day. As the saying goes, if you're playing the game and don't know who's the patsy, it's you. The great physicist Richard Feynman taught, "The first principle is that you must not fool yourself—and you are the easiest person to fool."

I'm calling System One your dog brain now because dogs are really quite trusting. They are easy to befriend. They eat pretty much anything put before them. Investing involves thinking more like a cat. Cats are quite circumspect about what they do and what they eat. That's why a cat has nine lives. Dogs have masters; cats have staff. If you want to prosper financially, think more like a cat, less like a dog.

Speaking of dogs and cats, cons exist in the animal world as well. I used to watch my little Maltese dog con my big German shepherd mix with ease. He just threw a fraudulent bark-fest at the living-room window. The Shepherd would drop the toy he'd stolen from the Maltese to race over and play police dog. Meanwhile, the Maltese scampered back, grabbed his toy, and hid. Chimpanzees con one another all the time

---

61 Robert Cialdini, *The Psychology of Persuasion* (New York: Harper Books, 2006).

too. And cons are funny: we laugh at the poor patsy as long as we don't think we're the patsy. The problem is the essence of a patsy requires that he or she doesn't know that he or she is a patsy. A patsy awakens to a con only after the patsy's been had. Even then, only slowly, long after the con artist is gone. The old traveling carnivals were cons. They were there to take in the yokels in the little towns they visited with displays and fakery, human oddities, and fearful demonstrations.

Local police were very wary of carnivals and sought to protect their citizens from predation. You can see this portrayed in one of the most devastating film noir, the littleseen *Nightmare Alley*,[62] with Tyrone Power cast against type. Or if you prefer a lighthearted, fun, and sanitized version of a traveling con artist, try *The Music Man*.[63]

Cons are big in mass entertainment. The most popular comedy duo in American history was Bud Abbott and Lou Costello. They were huge stars in the 1940s and 1950s on the radio and TV and in the movies. Abbott was dapper and slick, and was named one of the best-dressed men in Hollywood. Costello was fat, sloppy, and foolish, the rube, the child, and the patsy. In real life, Bud Abbott was born into a circus family and dropped out of school to spend his youth working the crowds as a barker at Dreamland Park in Coney Island. If you watch their routines, Abbott is doing what he was trained to do: constantly dupe and con Costello, ever credulous, into giving up his money or taking a dubious risk.

Bud's predations on Lou illustrate the workings of a con artist. When Bud slickers Lou out of money, he always, benevolently, offers him "a chance to get even!" He touts his own generosity and sympathy, as con artists always do. The "chance to get even" is always just another con. Typically, it is "Pick a number from one to ten." Costello picks four. Abbott snarls, "No, it was five, but you were close."[64] Costello loses his bet yet again. Often the bit allows Costello to get even in the end. In the real world of cons, lotteries, and casinos, that will never happen. Like Bud Abbott, casinos and lotteries cunningly let you feel close to winning. Lotteries now encourage you to choose

---

62 *Nightmare Alley*, Dir. Edmund Goulding, 20th Century Fox, 1947, Film.

63 *The Music Man*, Dir. Morton DaCosta, Warner Brothers, 1962, Film.

64 The Charity Bazaar, *The Abbott and Costello Show*, T.C.A. Productions, February 6, 1953.

your number for better play—because it's *your* lucky number, it's a sure winner. Slot machines with bigger and more frequent payouts beckon from the casino entrance to draw you in to play a less generous machine inside. Slots also have a lot of near wins—like two cherries out of three—built in to make your dog brain believe you barely missed out on that last treat.

Try again. Lose some more. Your dog brain cannot reckon the odds.

One of our greatest filmmakers is Martin Scorsese, and two of his best films are *Casino*[65] and *The Wolf of Wall Street*.[66] If you watch them both with a keen eye, undistracted by the glitz, glamour, sex, and violence, there are public-service announcements built into each film. The casinos of Las Vegas and the casino of Wall Street are built upon the hard-earned dollars of losing players!

How can you beat the casino? Don't go.

How can you beat the casino of Wall Street? Read on.

---

65 *Casino*, Dir. Martin Scorsese, Universal, 1995, Film.
66 *The Wolf of Wall Street*, Dir. Martin Scorsese, Red Granite Pictures, 2013, Film.

CHAPTER 8

The Wisdom of Diversification: Own the World—It Will Always Be Here

Human beings are linear thinkers by nature. We tend to perceive only one cause for one effect. We even like oneness for its own sake. TV reporters always give one reason for the stock market's movement each day. In reality there are innumerable reasons and much randomness, but no reporter dares report that. It is reality but it is not news. One cause, one effect. That is how we, as evolved creatures, are programmed to think. It is Isaac Bashevis Singer telling me that literature is not about masses, but about individuals.

We think in these simple linear ways about many things that in reality are far more complex and nuanced. We like to believe that there is but one love out there for each of us. As the Yiddish maxim teaches, "Every pot has its cover."

Irving Berlin wrote and Fred Astaire sang the love song, "I'm Putting All My Eggs in One Basket."[67] As the lyrics go, "I'm betting everything I've got on you." All love songs are about one person, the singer's one and only love. True love. Can you imagine a love song about sorting through a lot of lovers and putting eggs in many baskets? There are a few pop songs like that. "Kansas City,"[68] "California Girls."[69] But they aren't love songs, they're "fun" songs. As we discussed in chapter 1, we are wired to make one big bet and win it, in love and in life. Even if most of us lose those bets, nature wins, and nature wired us. And Irving Berlin knew how to sell a love song.

---

67   Irving Berlin, *I'm Putting All My Eggs in One Basket* (New York: Irving Berlin, 1936).

68   Jerry Lieber and Mike Stoller, *Kansas City* (New York: Sony/ATV, 1952).

69   Brian Wilson and Mike Love, *California Girls* (New York: Sony/ATV, 1965).

So need we ask why people love lotteries and playing the numbers, even as they lose and lose again, in the hope of one big win? It is part of our basic programming, our limited day-to-day common sense. But wouldn't we rather be rational and find a way to win our bets rather than lose them? Use System Two rather than System One. Uncommon sense rather than common sense.

Let's apply Charlie Munger's recommendation and invert: use Carl Jacobi's nineteenth-century mathematics, so effective in *It's a Wonderful Life* (chapter 6), and apply it to the state lottery. How can we make the lottery less random, less cruel, less exploitative of the innocents who pay into it and endlessly remake that same bad bet?

1. We could make it compulsory! It's less fun if you have to play and you cannot pick your number. Make every working adult play. Even the teenagers on summer jobs.
2. We could force you to buy a ticket every day, whether you have the money or not.
3. We could make the payoff small but certain; everybody wins so no one can lord it over anybody else.
4. We could delay the drawing until the players are old or sick!

Have you figured it out by now? Yes, it's Social Security! The program everyone hates to pay into but waits to collect and never disparages. The government program nobody loves to hate. Of course, no Social Security recipient feels anything like a lottery winner. There are no news stories about them. No grinning couples on camera holding up enlarged Social Security checks to wild applause.

Still, Social Security recipients have actually won the *unlottery*. A fair, rational, sane, and nonpredatory lottery. Most just don't know it. Not if they don't remember the United States before Social Security. Back when pneumonia was known as the old man's friend because it was better to be dead than poor, broke, cold, and old. People also don't know because it takes so long to get paid. Social Security is gratification delayed nearly unto death. Delayed gratification is something you need System Two to appreciate. Rational, not emotional thinking.

When you are young and paying into Social Security, you can't imagine ever getting the money back again. Young people who visit a retirement community or a nursing home cannot see these fragile elderly as their future selves any more than one could imagine an aged Elvis Presley or Marilyn Monroe. What they see are closer to zoo animals or a strange tribe they would never want to join. Why would they want to give their hard-earned dollars to help some old person they don't know yet, even if those old people are their future selves?

I am over sixty-five and entitled to receive Social Security, but I don't. I am delighted to defer it. Not just because the check will be larger when I do get it, but so I can feel younger by not receiving it! I don't want to win this unlottery yet!

So, at long last, how does all this relate to diversification, the subject of this chapter? I have come to diversification through a subterfuge. I wanted you to see how System One led you to want to win the state lottery and System Two could invert the state lottery into Social Security, where everybody wins. Now you can see how being rational about money is safer, wiser, and better than being emotional and irrational.

So let's turn to diversification.

Every age has its winning stocks, the stocks that, if you bought then, you'd be rich now. When I was a kid, it was Xerox—then it wasn't Xerox. Later it was Microsoft. Then it was Amazon and Apple. Now it's Google, Netflix, Amazon, Apple and Facebook. As we discuss in chapter 13, if you hitched a ride on one of these skyrockets, you could have gotten rich. (Full disclosure, I owned some Amazon but sold it at a good profit to install a generator. If I'd kept it, I could afford a hundred generators.) But the idea that you can, as appealing as it may be, is partly an illusion. It is very much the stuff of what the evolutionary psychologists call "hindsight bias." It's thinking that you could have known then what you know now. That's Monday-morning quarterbacking. That's looking at life in the rearview mirror. That's coulda, shoulda, woulda.

On my first day in physiology class at medical school, my professor announced: "We can explain anything. Sure! But what can we predict? If we cannot predict, our explanations are meaningless!" Think about it.

The comedian Jackie Mason has reformulated hindsight bias into a Jewish joke with a profound lesson in it. He assures us that "every Jew knows a building he could have bought thirty years ago for nine dollars." Then he proceeds to recall this familiar conversation:

"Do you know what that building is worth today? One hundred eighty-seven million!"

So Jackie asks this should-have-been real-estate tycoon, "Why don't you buy something now?"

"Now!" the "tycoon" gasps in exasperation at Jackie's naïveté. "Now is too late!"

And Jackie gets a big laugh at the expense of this self-deceiving schlemiel known to everyone. Never a successful real-estate owner, for obvious reasons.

The present is always far too late to buy a diamond in the rough with perfect hindsight. That is the essence of hindsight bias. Hindsight bias can convince you that you could have, should have, and would have known about that skyrocketing stock at the outset and that you would have bought it and sold it at just the right moments to become rich.

I cannot say it is a delusion because you *can* buy a skyrocketing stock and take profits. But I can comfortably say it is unwise to pin your hopes and dreams on that idea. You are statistically unlikely to find the next Amazon, buy it, sell it at the right moment, diversify, and keep the wealth. That is System One talking.

But why try to find a proverbial needle in the haystack? Isn't it simpler and more effective to buy the haystack? Remember, this is your future and the future of your family we're talking about.

Let's go to System Two, uncommon sense, and approach this question rationally. Yes, we would all like to participate in the success of skyrocketing stocks. We would like to believe we could spot them, buy them, and grow rich. But rationally, we have to consider, setting aside our pride, narcissism, and overconfidence, that we probably won't do it or won't do it often enough to make it a winning strategy.

I've already discussed the dopamine rush of picking winners, how we overestimate our ability to pick winners, and how picking winners is very often a loser's game. Among stocks there are always more losers than winners, and many winners end up losers eventually.

Look at history. Once the winner was Greece, home of the greatest philosophers, warriors, and scientists. Today it is the poor man of Europe. Rome held an empire, but it is now shrunken and below replacement-level reproduction. German music, art, literature, science, and military might were brought to ashes, and then the country came back again as the industrial powerhouse of Europe. Russian Communism promised heaven on earth, ended in ignominious collapse after seventy years of misery, and the country is now ruled by an oligarchy.

Examine the Dow stocks of yesteryear, so few of which are in the Dow today.

Individual winning stocks are often ephemeral. The commonsense perception of them is that they are winning, and the rational, long-term reality is that they rise and fall. But there is a long-term winner—humanity at large. The world is always growing, and the world is winning: more people, more science, more production, more knowledge, and more wisdom.

That is the rule of life and the rule of wealth.

Think it through. Which is the better bet, an individual NFL team or the National Football League? Teams win and lose, but professional football endures. Should you bet on an individual television show, a television network, the television industry, or the entertainment sector as a whole? TV is dying, but entertainment thrives. Each time, the very unexciting, uncompelling, but rational answer is the broader group, the wider net, and the whole shebang is the safer bet.

The best way to grow wealthy is slowly, through a diversified portfolio of stocks in a low-cost index fund, so that the growth of every winner is in your portfolio and you receive a fair share of market gains. This is the philosophy of Jack Bogle, the founder of the Vanguard Funds, who you'll read about in chapter 12. For those who insist upon the challenge of investing in individual stocks, Jack Bogle makes the following suggestion: allot a small percentage of your wealth to individual stocks and tally the results fairly, accurately, and completely lest you fall prey to a biased memory. See if the index fund does not do better!

I have owned index funds and individual stocks, the latter far more often and far longer. Full disclosure, I would have done better over the many decades with index funds.

Finally, I have many patients and have seen too many through life's tragedies.

The worst tragedies are the avoidable ones. The financial casualties among my patients have largely occurred in the markets. Some found their tragedies by taking unreasonable risks: playing options and commodities or buying on margin, but most poignantly by failing to diversify their investments and by relying upon a single stock, bond, or sector. So, when their investments went south, they too were destroyed.

The best cinematic example of failure to diversify is the O'Hara family in *Gone with the Wind*.

Scarlett comes home to Tara, sacked and plundered in the Civil War. Her father, Gerald, widowed and demented, is perusing his life savings. What follows below is the scene as written in the original screenplay:

Scarlett: "What are those papers?"

Gerald: "Oh...(looks at them as if seeing them for the first time). Bonds—they're all we've saved—all we have left—bonds."

Scarlett (hopefully): "What kind of bonds, Pa?"

Gerald: "Why, Confederate bonds, of course, daughter."

Scarlett (sharply): "Confederate bonds! What good are they to anybody?"

Gerald (with a flash of his old peremptory manner): "I'll not have you talking like that, Katie Scarlett!"

Scarlett (dismayed): "Oh, Pa, what are we going to do with no money—nothing to eat."

Gerald: (confused and hurt like a small boy): "We must ask your mother." (as though he has made a discovery) "That's it...We must ask Mrs. O'Hara."

Scarlett (startled): "Ask...Mother?" A look of horror comes over her face as she realizes for the first time that her father's mind is gone.[70]

And it dawns upon poor Scarlett that it is up to her to save Tara. It makes great drama because it is so realistic. So many people have a "can't fail" investment that is so good they need not diversify until the unimaginable happens and it is suddenly too late.

Remember Machiavelli's sound advice that no one looking at calm waters anticipates a storm, just as innocent Scarlett does not anticipate the collapse of her world at the opening of *Gone with the Wind*.

---

70 www.dailyscript.com/scripts/Gone_With_the_Wind.pdf, p126. (accessed September 17, 2017).

CHAPTER 9

The Richest Man in Babylon: The Bible Story Not Found in the Bible

*T*he Richest Man in Babylon[71] is the most instructive Bible story you won't find in the Bible. It's a get-rich-slowly story that, if you take it to heart and live it, will serve you and your family forever. It's the first of a set of parables about how to manage money over your lifetime. Beyond that, it incorporates many ideas discussed in this book and makes them memorable so you can think them and live them every day. Journalists know we remember stories best and numbers and ideas less well.

The Richest Man in Babylon was written by George S. Clason, an American author whose first careers were as a mapmaker and an entrepreneur. He published the original road atlas of the United States, no small feat. He penned *The Richest Man in Babylon* parables and other stories as pamphlets for distribution at banks across the country. He later compiled them into a book. They are still available as a book and are now free on the web, are illustrated, and appear animated in YouTube videos, which may help you to digest them and keep them in mind.[72]

Clason set his stories in ancient Babylon because the Babylonians were among the earliest originators and inventors of money, perhaps six thousand years ago. We think of money as just as natural as air and water, but it is really an invention. We value it by association, for what it buys: food, shelter, and material possessions.

---

71 George S. Clason, *The Richest Man in Babylon* (New York: Signet, 1988).

72 http://www.youtube.com/watch?v=HDAcinedh78 (accessed September 17, 2017).

Accumulated as wealth, money brings power, independence, and safety as well as freedom from want, fear, and subservience. Charlie Munger and Warren Buffett always say they wanted to be rich so they could be independent.[73] As Clason teaches, in the intervening six thousand years, the rules of money have not changed.

Long story short: Bansir the chariot maker is old and tired and has begun to resist his very difficult work. He is visited by his old friend Kobbi the musician. Both are highly competent in their fields, but they are both broke. They squabble over a small loan. Then they recall their childhood friend, Arkad, said now to be the richest man in Babylon. They resolve to visit him and learn his secret if he will tell them.

Arkad receives his old friends and is happy to share his secret. Arkad is neither cheap nor greedy, and he is not smarter or harder working than his old friends. So how did he amass his wealth? He learned his secret from a wealthy old man for whom he worked, and then he applied it. The secret is this: "A part of all I earn is mine to keep."[74] Or simply said, "Pay yourself first."[75] Set aside 10 percent or more of your earnings and put them in a safe investment at a reasonable return, and you will surely grow rich over your lifetime. "Wealth, like a tree, grows from a tiny seed."[76] The earlier it is planted, the bigger it will grow in your lifetime. Then you will bask beneath the tree and enjoy both shade and fruit and no longer labor for your money.

Simple! So simple that very bright people foolishly miss it. It is the very same lesson that two academics, Thomas Stanley and William Danko, learned and taught in their book, *The Millionaire Next Door.*[77] The whole concept can be simply summarized in two contrasting portraits: the humble, honest salaried person earns $100,000 a year, lives simply, remains married, and saves and invests 10 to 20 percent of his or her income over a working lifetime and becomes a millionaire over time. Contrast that life

---

73 theinvestmentsblog.blogspot.com/2009/11/miscellaneous-munger-quotes.html (accessed September 17, 2017)

74 Clason, *The Richest Man in Babylon*, 17.

75 Ibid., 18.

76 Ibid., 19.

77 Thomas J. Stanley and William D. Danko, *The Millionaire Next Door: The Surprising Secrets of America's Wealthy* (New York: Gallery Books, 1998).

with the bold surgeon earning $700,000 a year who lives life in a great big way—having mansions and sports cars, divorcing and remarrying freely, spending wildly and saving minimally, if at all—and ends life broke and angry.

I have seen it in my office, and I have seen it in my life. I have seen simple people obey the rules of wealth and grow wealthy and smart people ignore them and end up poor. Charlie Munger and Warren Buffett will teach you to become rich slowly, by just not being foolish enough to violate these eternal principles against your better judgment. The people I have met who earned big and ended up poor say the same thing: "We never thought it would end." They thought the huge income would never stop and would last them their lives. But fashions change. Lawyers lose their partnerships and are ushered out of failing firms; surgeons and physicians are forcibly retired under HMO rules or lose their skills or their backs give out. Executives are drummed out at fifty-five and cannot find commensurate work.

Lorenz Hart, the brilliant tragic lyricist, first partner of Richard Rodgers, wrote these poignant lyrics for the rarely sung reprise of "Bewitched, Bothered and Bewildered"[78] from *Pal Joey*:

Burned a lot
But learned a lot
And now you are broke, though you earned a lot.
Bewitched, bothered and bewildered, no more.

Who knows better about earning a lot and ending up broke than show people!

To be sure, there is a well-worn objection to Arkad's prescription for wealth. It is the cry, "I can barely get by on what I make now!" Arkad has a simple retort: "Now I will tell a strange truth, the reason for which I know not. When I ceased to pay out more than nine tenths of my earnings, I managed to get along just as well."[79]

---

78 Richard Rodgers and Lorenz Hart, *Bewitched, Bothered and Bewildered* (New York: Chappell & Co., 1941).

79 Clason, *The Richest Man in Babylon*, 36.

We know this is true. When workers have automatic savings deductions, they never miss them and live much the same. If they receive that money as pay, they spend it. Even a homeless person could save five dollars per day by drinking water instead of beverages. Plug that into the online Compounding Monkey[80] and check out the return at the 7 percent market rate over fifty years: $793,849 compounded annually!

Incredible, of course. So convince yourself as my organic chemistry professor advised students so many years ago.

---

80 www.moneychimp.com/calculator/compound_interest_calculator.htm (accessed September 17, 2017).

PART IV

Learning From Money Masters

CHAPTER 10

Vanguard's Jack Bogle:
The George Bailey of Investing

In chapter 8 I said there really is a force of nature as powerful as the Force in *Star Wars*. Movie magic can reflect reality. In this chapter I introduce you to a real-life financier who champions common investors as George Bailey championed the homeowners of Bedford Falls when he built Bailey Park in *It's a Wonderful Life*! This financier has no heavenly assistance, and though he has had his share of reversals, he never, to public knowledge, reached the end of his rope. There will never be a movie about him, except perhaps a documentary, because his story is not dramatic. But his story is well worth telling to every investor everywhere.

His name is John C. (Jack) Bogle, and he was born in 1929. Like most men of his generation—such as Warren Buffett and Charlie Munger, who I profile later—Jack Bogle and his family were greatly affected by the Great Depression of the 1930s. Men of this vintage know what misery poverty and even near-poverty can bring and what comforts even modest prosperity affords.

Jack Bogle attended Princeton University and studied economics, graduating magna cum laude. His senior thesis was entitled, "The Economic Role of the Investment Company," and his investing philosophy guided his entire working life. Jack Bogle developed the index mutual fund, perhaps the single most profound idea in investing, certainly the most significant for the general public. The index mutual fund allows even the humblest individual investor to participate in the nearly boundless success of corporate America for a fraction of the cost of any other investing vehicle and without the risk of picking individual stocks.

Jack Bogle began his career at Wellington Management, where he climbed the ladder of success from 1951 until 1974, when he left to found the Vanguard Group. There he championed the first low-cost, no-load (a load is an entry fee—note the euphemism) mutual funds based upon market indices. There would be no stock picking and no stock trading except as necessary to maintain correlations with the market indices—just passive and super-low-cost investing.

Now this was not exclusively Jack Bogle's idea. It was a natural outgrowth of the efficient market hypothesis (EMH). The EMH, put simply, says that rather than try to beat the market, you should just buy the market because the market, in its wisdom, has every bit of information already factored in. The EMH is the product of research by a number of financial and economic theorists, most prominently Eugene Fama, who won a third share of a Nobel Prize for his work in 2013.

Now, is the EMH true? Is the market actually completely efficient? If it is, how can we explain tulip mania in Holland? The South Sea bubble? Enron? Bear Stearns and Lehman Brothers? Where was the efficient market then? And so many other times in market bubbles and meltdowns? How could Berkshire Hathaway beat the market year after year if the market is totally efficient? Obviously, it's not.

Can you win a Nobel Prize for an erroneous idea? Sure! A neurologist, Egas Moniz, won a Nobel Prize in medicine in 1949 for pioneering the prefrontal lobotomy as a treatment for psychosis, a procedure that today is one of the most reviled and horrific errors in the history of health care. The Nobel Peace Prize has been given to warmongers for whom it was little more than a good conduct medal as a reward for a little peace!

But there are workable hypotheses that are not absolutely true. We call alcoholism a disease. If it's a disease, how can I explain my alcoholic patient who crashed a car due to drunk driving and simply stopped drinking forever? He never touched another drop after I told him not to. I'm no Svengali. Plenty of other alcoholics keep right on drinking, even as their relatives die of alcoholism. But an alcoholic's best hope for recovery is Alcoholics Anonymous combined with the medical disease model.

The disease model of alcoholism is far from a perfect fit.

Alcoholism is not pneumonia or cancer. Comedian Dom Irrera says he would like to be alcoholic so he could binge and be congratulated whenever he cares to stop drinking. But the disease model of alcoholism is a working hypothesis that undercuts alcoholics' deep shame at their behavior and the pain it causes to others and grants doctors the medical tools to help alcoholics resist the lure of alcohol.

We cannot ignore workable but imperfect models. We cannot let the perfect be the enemy of the good. The Gershwin Brothers wrote, "It Ain't Necessarily So."[81] But followers of the Abrahamic religions don't toss the Bible for lack of a real-life talking snake.

Well, does the EMH work in practice?

Does it ever! The Vanguard S&P 500 Fund (VOO) regularly beats at least 85 percent of all the managed funds every year, despite all their research and supposed market wisdom. It even beats hedge funds, as Warren Buffett proved in the famous bet I discussed in chapter 1. I have owned Vanguard Exchange Traded Funds and watched them gently and surely rise as the rest of my stock portfolio wends its rocky way north, with considerably more reversals and collapses, worry, and head-shaking regrets.

How was Jack Bogie's idea received by the larger financial community? How are new ideas generally welcomed? Like another Gershwin song, "They All Laughed,"[82] and worse. The financial world greeted index funds with curses and ill wishes befitting anything that threatens one's livelihood. Vanguard was called "Bogle's Folly," and Bogle personally was called a fool, a Marxist, and a Communist! This to a dyed-in-thewool old-school Republican!

How has the competition played out? Vanguard today is the largest mutual-fund organization in the world, with more than $4 trillion—yes, *trillion*—under

---

81 George Gershwin and Ira Gershwin, *It Ain't Necessarily So* (New York: Chappell & Co., 1935).

82 George Gershwin and Ira Gershwin, *They All Laughed* (New York: Chappell & Co., 1937).

management. After forty years, Jack Bogle has proven his point. In Warren Buffett's annual Berkshire Hathaway letter of 2016, he called Jack Bogle a hero and wrote:

> "If a statue is ever erected to honor the person who has done the most for American investors, the hands-down choice should be Jack Bogle. For decades, Jack has urged investors to invest in ultra-low-cost index funds. In his crusade, he amassed only a tiny percentage of the wealth that has typically flowed to managers who have promised their investors large rewards while delivering them nothing—or, as in our bet, less than nothing—of added value."[83]

It is well known that Jack Bogle, whose net worth is estimated at $80 million, could have been a billionaire many times over. That he chose not to be but to build Vanguard as a mutual fund owned by the fundholders is a testament to his character and purpose. Like George Bailey in the mythical Bedford Falls, in the real world of finance, Jack Bogle is truly the richest man in town.

---

83 Berkshire Hathaway Annual Letter to Shareholders, p. 16, www.berkshirehathaway.com/letters/2016ltr.pdf.

CHAPTER 11

Warren Buffett:
The Oracle of Omaha

What can you say about a man of relatively humble beginnings, possessed of a keen mathematical intellect and relentless drive, who sought and accumulated financial and worldly wisdom, built a corporate colossus, compounded the wealth of himself and his investors into the billions, became the richest man in the world, shared his unvarnished wisdom with the world throughout his business life, and, in the December of his years, gave all his money away? What can you say?

A thank-you just won't cover it.

Remember that plaque on George Bailey's wall: "All you can take with you is that which you have given away." How many of us can live up to that? Warren Buffett has.

He was born and bred in Omaha, Nebraska, in the first year of the Great Depression, 1930. You learn about money fast when there isn't any. As a small boy, he was fascinated by numbers and collecting, and he learned the lessons of compounding from an early age. His mother, who was also supremely numerate, sang him a song about it. (Warren Buffett plays the ukulele and sings too. But I have yet to hear the compounding song.)

He worked hard, even as a boy, delivering newspapers and buying and selling soda pop. He bought his first share of stock at age eleven and never stopped buying. As a boy, he swore to become a millionaire, and by age thirty he fulfilled that dream. His primary mentor was Benjamin Graham, a professor at Columbia

University's School of Business, whose *The Intelligent Investor*[84] and *Security Analysis*[85] were Warren Buffett's bibles.

He learned to find undervalued companies—cigar butts, he called them, with a single puff left. One of them, a failing textile company, Berkshire Hathaway, was to become legendary years later as the greatest investment opportunity in human history. From Graham's philosophy, in partnership with Charlie Munger (see chapter 12), he expanded his thinking to acquiring better quality businesses, purchased in part or in toto, at better-than-bargain prices, always compounding the earnings and never declaring a dividend.

Unfailingly polite, relentlessly critical of Wall Street abuses and excesses, he has been a beacon and a boon to investors everywhere, more so to his shareholders, many of whom attend his annual "Woodstock for Capitalists" in Omaha. There, he and Charlie Munger hold forth for hours before the faithful shareholders assembled to share his wisdom. As Charlie Munger has pointed out, these people are not drawn to Omaha to visit their money or celebrate their success; they can do that with a statement. Berkshire Hathaway shareholders feel they have participated in a minor miracle—the slow accumulation of wealth and wisdom over a lifetime. They rarely sell. (Full disclosure: I have only bought, albeit not early enough.) Berkshire Hathaway's average gain since 1965 has been 20 percent; the S&P 500's gain has been 10 percent. Try 10 percent versus 20 percent for any sum in an online compounder and amaze yourself. Buffett freely confesses it is mathematically impossible to carry that rate of return forward. Berkshire is just too big for any new acquisition to move the needle. But Berkshire shareholders can look forward to steady returns, though still with no dividends as yet.

Probably, the single best introduction to Warren Buffett's life is the HBO biography currently available online at HBO: *Becoming Warren Buffett.*[86] His life has been

---

84 Benjamin Graham, *The Intelligent Investor* (New York: HarperBusiness, 2006).

85 Benjamin Graham and David Dodd, *Security Analysis* (New York: McGraw-Hill Education, 2008).

86 www.hbo.com/documentaries/becoming-warren-buffett (accessed September 17, 2017)

chronicled in *The Snowball: Warren Buffett and the Business of Life* by Alice Schroeder.[87] His philosophy and his thinking can best be gleaned from the annual Berkshire Hathaway letters, which are collected in book form but immediately accessible free on the web at the Berkshire Hathaway website. Eagerly awaited by the entire investing world, the letters appear online and arrive in the mail to shareholders every spring. Homespun, candid, frank, honest, and forthright, thoroughly Midwestern in spirit and demeanor, these annual letters are insightful, amusing, and entertaining. In a financial world that has more than its share of deception and manipulation, it is a welcome breath of spring every spring.

There are many other Warren Buffett interviews and speeches online, all well worth viewing.

At my dinner with Isaac Bashevis Singer, I said a very foolish thing I do not like to recall. I was young. When he told me one must never deal with masses in literature, I foolishly pointed out that he once did precisely that in one of his stories. He scolded me. "What do you expect me to do? Push my own merchandise?" Warren Buffett follows the same policy. He does not recommend his own merchandise: Berkshire Hathaway stock. He recommends low-cost index funds. Heed the advice of the great man himself:

> When trillions of dollars are managed by Wall Streeters charging high fees, it will usually be the managers who reap outsized profits, not the clients. Both large and small investors should stick with low-cost index funds.[88]

Give all your billions away, and speak truth to power. Who can naysay that?

---

87 Alice Schroeder, *The Snowball: Warren Buffett and the Business of Life* (New York: Bantam Books, 2009).

88 https://www.forbes.com/sites/johnwasik/2017/03/01/warren-buffets-single-best-piece-of-advice/#60211b6c4169 (accessed September 17, 2017).

CHAPTER 12

Charlie Munger: The Sage of Omaha

Reading and listening to Warren Buffett will doubtless make you a better investor. Reading and listening to his partner, Charlie Munger, will not only make you a better investor, it will also make you a better thinker, a better spouse, a better parent, a better friend, and a better person.

Charlie Munger is one of the deepest, fastest, and most penetrating thinkers I have ever encountered on audio, on video, or in print. He is, at this writing, ninety-three, and his skills are undiminished. No single individual, living or dead, has taught me more about investing, science, and life than this remarkable man.

His education is very broad, and he never stops learning. His formal education consists of undergraduate coursework at Caltech and the University of Michigan—no undergraduate degree—and a Juris Doctor from Harvard, *magna cum laude*. He laments his professed ignorance daily and reads relentlessly. He sits on corporate and hospital boards. He has run a hospital. He ran a successful law practice that thrives and bears his name to this day. He has run the prototype of a hedge fund with stunning success. He has been cochair of Berkshire Hathaway for decades and, with its founder, Warren Buffett, adapted its investment philosophy to scale up from millions to billions while still beating the markets. His lecture, "The Psychology of Human Misjudgment,"[89] available online in dozens of incarnations, is the finest single lecture about the human mind I have ever heard, and it came from a man who has never

---

89 http://www.youtube.com/watch?v=pqzcCfUglws (accessed September 17, 2017). www.hb.org/the-psychology-of-human-misjudgment-by-charles-t-munger/(accessed September 17, 2017).

taken a psychology course in his life. I have listened to it again and again and never retained all of its counterintuitive wisdom, which, like Freud's jokes and dreams, easily escapes one's mind. One hedge-fund manager is said to have heard it every day for over a year as he drove to work.

Charlie Munger does not suffer fools; he is as blunt as he is sharp, and he has nurtured his modicum of tact only late in his life. As he has said, "People hated me."[90] Unvarnished rationality is often embarrassing and unwelcome. Charlie Munger credits his lifelong success not to native intelligence but to rationality and "a long attention span."[91]

Charlie Munger has suffered. He recounts his life failures freely. He has lost a son, and he has lost an eye. He is wildly averse to self-pity. He is a student of the Greek slave philosopher, Epictetus, and counsels that every adversity is an opportunity to behave well. Charlie Munger warns that life will have numerous blows, unfair blows, and that to suffer them with grace and dignity is a duty. He warns against obsessive love and recommends "admiration-based love," just as he seeks the "web of trust," described in chapter 6, born of repeated mutual experiences of trust and fair play among colleagues and coworkers. He and Warren Buffett warn that a reputation built over a lifetime can be destroyed in five minutes. He counsels ethical behavior not only because it is right, but because it works best.[92]

Charlie Munger warns of the dangers of a life guided by envy. He and Warren Buffett agree that envy, not greed, drives the world.[93] As Charlie Munger notes, modern psychology barely addresses envy and jealousy, yet they are all over the Ten Commandments.[94] As a premedical student at Columbia, I had to be fiercely com-

---

90   https://medium.com/personal-growth/charlie-munger-on-the-intelligent-improvement-of-yourself-662be039c891(accessed September 17, 2017).

91   https://www.farnamstreetblog.com/2017/02/charlie-munger-wisdom/(accessed September 17, 2017).

92   https://25iq.com/2015/10/24/a-dozen-things-ive-learned-from-charlie-munger-about-ethics/ (accessed September 17, 2017).

93   https://consilientinterest.com/2013/09/06/quote-from-warren-buffett-about-greed-and-envy/ (accessed September 17, 2017)

94   David Clark, *The Tao of Charlie Munger: A Compilation of Quotes from Berkshire Hathaway's Vice Chairman on Life, Business and the Pursuit of Wealth with Commentary by David Clark* (New York:

petitive and wildly jealous to ace my courses and be admitted to a US medical school. Once in school, I soon learned that someone else would always be smarter than me, and I soon learned that that was just fine. I would learn at my own pace.

Charlie Munger counsels that someone will always be getting richer faster than you, and that is fine as well.[95] He's right, as usual.

Charlie Munger does not observe professional boundaries. If an idea in science, math, law, or medicine helps solve the problem he faces, he borrows freely. He believes in mathematical inversion as an approach to the seemingly unsolvable, a method George Bailey's guardian angel, Clarence, uses in *It's a Wonderful Life*. If Charlie Munger wants to better a situation, he first thinks how to worsen it, just as Clarence does for George. So he preaches, if you want to ruin your life, be unreliable. "You'll crater immediately."[96] If you want to ruin your finances, live beyond your means, as Mozart did, and live in the misery of overwhelming debt.[97]

Charlie Munger recommends "lifetime learning" so that your mind is ever expanding and ever reaching, a compounding of your own intellect fed by experience and reading. He urges us to go to bed wiser than when we woke up. He reads biographies voraciously and recommends spending time with "the eminent dead" through their writings. They are always there in easy reach, he reminds us.[98]

Charlie Munger is a student of Ben Franklin and the ancient Greeks. A compendium of his "greatest hits," his lectures and essays, is entitled, in memory of Franklin, *Poor Charlie's Almanack*.[99] It is a weighty tome, big and unwieldy and expensive to

Scribner, 2017), 192.

95   https:www.gurufocus.com/news/336885/charlie-munger-on-how-to-be-happy-get-rich-and-other-advice(accessed September 17, 2017).

96   https://www.farnamstreetblog.com/2016/04/munger-operating-system/(accessed September 17, 2017).

97   www.businessinsider.com/charlie-munger-quotes-investing-things-2016-1/#if-mozart-couldn't-get-away-with-it-neither-can-you-15 (accessed September 17, 2017).

98   https://www.farnamstreetblog.com/2016/05/Seneca-eminent-dead/(accessed September 17, 2017).

99   Kaufman, ed., *Poor Charlie's Alamanck*.

boot, though the profits go to charity. It's the best sixty dollars you will ever spend. If you don't find it gratifying, take Charlie's advice about another book (not his own) and "give it to a more intelligent friend."[100]

Had I never heard and read Charles T. Munger, I could never have written this book. He has been both an inspiration and an education. Once you have heard and read him, you can never think narrowly again. One of his inspirations is Albert Einstein, who famously said, "Everything should be made as simple as possible, but not simpler."[101] The Munger application, which we previously encountered in chapter 6, has given us the "fundamental algorithm of life":

Repeat What Works!

Think about it! It explains just about every form of success in life. From evolution to the stock market. It has an obvious corollary—stop what does not work. So simple and yet so difficult. As the US Marine Corps' rock 'n' roll group, the Essex, sang in 1963, "Easier, easier said than done."[102] Because people tend to do what they are accustomed to doing, whether it works or not. The force of habit. But habits, like common sense, are malleable. You can change your habits if you only try.[103] The whole country has—from smokers to nonsmokers in a generation!

So how can we repeat what works in becoming rich over a lifetime?

1.   Live within your means.
2.   Invest the savings in low-cost index funds.
3.   Compound all your life.

---

100   boards.fool.com/charlie-munger-in-rare-form-20741250.aspx?sort=username(accessed September 17, 2017).

101   https://www.brainyquote.com/quotes/quotes/a/alberteins103652.html (accessed September 17, 2017).

102   William Linton and Larry Huff, *Easier Said Than Done* (Nashville, TN: EMI Longitude Music Company, 1962).

103   Charles Duhigg, *The Power of Habit: Why We Do What We Do in Life and Business* (New York: Random House Trade Paperbacks, 2014).

What does not work?

1. Living beyond your means and compounding debt.
2. Gambling in casinos, lotteries, or markets.
3. Addictions to alcohol, drugs, sex, or risk.

At this point I hope you can join me in saying about these simple concepts, as Charlie Munger says about betting, "To me, it's obvious that the winner has to bet very selectively. It's been obvious to me since very early in life. I don't know why it's not obvious to very many other people."[104]

I sincerely hope that all of this is now obvious to you.

---

104 https://quotefancy.com/quote/1562177/Charlie-Munger-to-me-it-s-obvious-that-the-winner-has-to-bet-very-selectively-it's-been (accessed September 17, 2017) .

PART V

Dare To Risk Your Money

CHAPTER 13

Individual Stocks: Mispriced Bets, Skyrockets, and Blood in the Streets

I f you still insist on purchasing individual stocks—after all I have discussed about diversification; the failure of most investors, even the pros, to beat the market indices; the impossibility of consistently timing the market on the way in and the way out; and the likelihood that many of the people who beat the market have done so randomly and will lose it back randomly—what should you do?

First, never risk it all. People like to bet the farm, "put the whole bundle on Greased Lightning," as Tony Curtis says in *Some Like It Hot*, in the hope that by casting their fate to the wind, Dame Fortune will smile upon them, and they'll win big.[105]

Snare and delusion. Never risk what you need. As Jack Bogle teaches, invest most of your money safely, in low-cost index funds that beat 85 percent of all managed funds. Think about it. You can get a grade of 85 percent, a B+ in investing, with no effort. Work harder and buy individual stocks, and you will likely lower your grade to a C, or you may even flunk Investing 101. So why even try? In school if you work harder, your grades go up. In the market, they usually go down. Better put the same effort into earning more money to invest in your index funds. Warren Buffett recommends Vanguard. It's the better bet.

If you still insist on taking the plunge, how do you proceed?

---

105 *Some Like It Hot,* Dir. Billy Wilder.

Well, be aware that wise investors and even wiser horse players *rarely bet, and only when the odds are in their favor*. Charlie Munger advises searching long and hard for "the mispriced bet," the rare times when the efficient market hypothesis runs off the rails or the "madness of crowds" offers you a contrarian opportunity to buy a solid stock at a depressed price.[106] This may occur in a market rout or amid a flood of bad news about a previously well-regarded and reliable corporation. The sage pronouncement attributed to Baron Rothschild is "Buy when there's blood in the streets, even if the blood is your own."[107]

Buying when there is blood in the street is very hard to do! Blood is transfixing. There is a perhaps apocryphal story of a health-care teacher throwing "blood" on the floor of the classroom and asking students how much "blood" they see. Students universally overestimate the amount.

How could it be easier to buy when blood is in the streets? Go back to Einstein. Use a thought experiment. Think of yourself as a doctor or a nurse tending to a sick and wounded but excellent stock, which you can heal by bringing it under your care, doing good and doing well at the same time. I did that with Bank of America during the financial crisis of 2008 and 2009 with the well-known result.

My very kind bookkeeper—I call him my CFO!—thinks of low prices on good stocks as sale prices. Recessions and market drops are the time to pick up some bargains! Of course it's unsettling to buy when no one else is buying. And maybe you feel foolish buying when the crowd is selling or hiding. So use this thought experiment: good stocks are on sale, and you're privileged enough to get in the store early, before it's open to the public.

In *It's a Wonderful Life*, the nefarious Mr. Potter is "picking up some bargains" when the Great Depression hits Bedford Falls: he buys the bus line, the department stores, and the bank. You don't have to be evil to buy in a crash, just be smart.

---

106 https://seekingalpha.com/article/4034622-u-s-bank-valuations-time-think-like-charlie-munger(accessed September 17, 2017).

107 https://www.forbes.com/2009/02/23/contrarian-markets-boeing-personal-finance_investopedia.html (accessed September 17, 2017).

Horrific to contemplate but stock in The Boeing Company, the aircraft manufacturer, fell for a year after the events of 9/11 and then rose 400 percent over the next five years.

Sir John Templeton, fabled investor, recommended buying "at the point of maximum pessimism."[108]

Remember too the words of Nobel laureate Rudyard Kipling in his poem "If," which was a message to his son, John, on how to succeed in life: "If you can keep your head when all about you are losing theirs and blaming it on you...you'll be a Man my son!"[109]

The big risk, of course, in buying a collapsing stock is that you have actually grabbed a falling knife, or worse, a falling sword, and bleed out money as a consequence. No one can predict when the price of any stock has bottomed out.

It requires a strong stomach to hold a stock that has fallen below the purchase price, sit, and anticipate a subsequent recovery months or even years later. And sometimes the stock never recovers! Some contrarian investors were buying Lehman Brothers and Bear Stearns as the shares went south for good. Seasoned market watchers often suggest waiting until a beaten-down stock begins to rise again before you buy. But beware of what Wall Streeters call a *dead-cat bounce*, when a hopelessly depressed stock achieves a brief and perhaps manipulated rise before death ensues.

Also, you don't want to buy just anything that's beaten down. What are the standards for a stock that Berkshire Hathaway buys? Warren Buffett and Charlie Munger have articulated their standards:

1. Only buy what you understand and is within your circle of competence.
2. Buy companies run by able and trustworthy people.

---

108   www.telegraph.co.uk/finance/personalfinance/investing/10644238/How-to-invest-like-...-Sir-John-Templeton.html (accessed September 17, 2017).

109   https://en.wikipedia.org/wiki/If--(accessed September 17, 2017).

3. Buy stocks that have a proven track record of dividends, which shows *proven durability*.
4. Buy stocks that have what Warren Buffett calls a wide moat, a castle's moat, so the corporate castle can't be easily invaded by sharp competitors; that predicts *future durability*.
5. Only buy at an attractive price. Remember the Nifty Fifty.[110]

Some investors prefer to bet on a rising star that does not fulfill any of these wise requirements. Everyone knows someone who hitched a ride on one of the sky-rockets of the new millennium: Apple, Amazon, Facebook, Netflix, or Google. And who can argue with success? If you have known, admired, and researched a company, buying its publicly traded stock is probably not an unreasonable thing to do if you do your homework and don't bet the farm. My own favorites have been Amazon and Costco, as I have used and been delighted with the services of both. I have been amply rewarded by both the stocks and the purchases. That is not a recommendation but a recollection. I cannot and do not suggest any individual stocks or individual stock buying in this book.

The single most unwise practice is innocently buying stocks touted by a friend, a neighbor, or a telephone solicitation as the next new thing. You can then fall prey to the notorious "pump and dump," a well-worn Wall Street scam best portrayed in two well-known movies: *Boiler Room*[111] and *The Wolf of Wall Street*.[112]

Here's the scam: drum up interest in a dubious stock you bought low for yourself, and then pump it to the patsies. Watch it rise, and then sell out at the top, enjoying profits galore. The "dump" occurs when the stock then loses support, falls, and crushes the patsies.

I grew up in two little neighborhoods in an outer borough of New York City. A pump and dump was pulled in each one. I asked a good friend of the family how

---

110 www.businessinsider.com/warren-buffetts-4-investing-principles-2016-1 (accessed September 17, 2017).

111 *Boiler Room*, Dir. Ben Younger, New Line Cinema, 2000, Film.

112 *The Wolf of Wall Street*, Dir. Martin Scorsese.

anyone could do such a terrible thing. He grew up in mean streets and gave me the street answer: "Who are you going to screw, if not your friends?"

The lesson is this: if you should buy individual stocks, prepare by learning. Both Warren Buffett and Charlie Munger urge you to read. Both of them read all day, every day. Charlie Munger says he knows no wise person who does not read. Read and learn—math, science, biography, history, politics, and so on. Expand yourself and your understanding of the world. As Charlie Munger teaches, go to bed smarter than you woke up. If you do that, as you grow, as a person and as an investor, you will be better able to spot the anomalies, exploit the inefficiencies, anticipate the trends, and buy the right stocks at the right times, if you dare even try.

When I was growing up in the 1950s, my public school had a savings program for the students run by the local bank. Each of us got a passbook, and the pennies we deposited each week accumulated and drew interest over the years. That was my first lesson in the accumulation and compounding of money. I remember when I reached $280.00, my parents agreed to allow me to withdraw it and buy the vaunted *Encyclopedia Britannica*, the compendium of worldly wisdom that was the gold standard of the day among ordinary Americans. I remember when the huge and heavy set arrived in twenty-four volumes: the look, the smell, the feel of the paper, the faux-leather jackets, and the gold print on the bindings. That was my first lesson in how the accumulation and compounding of money could lead to knowledge and independence. I could now read the *Britannica* at my leisure, in my home, and at my pace.

The twenty-four volumes of the Britannica sit now, unused for decades, in my basement. Call me a hoarder, but I cannot throw them out. Yet they yield so little compared to the treasure trove of free wisdom available on the web, updated and expanding constantly like an educational universe!

Where have I learned the most on the web about investing? I will offer a small list to the reader, with gratitude and good wishes:

Warren Buffett: his annual letters at the Berkshire Hathaway site, www.berkshire-hathaway.com/letters/letters.html.

Charlie Munger: "The Psychology of Human Misjudgment," at https://www.hb.org/the-psychology-of-human-misjudgment-by-charles-t-munger//.

The Farnam Street Blog maintained by Shane Parrish, available at the website, https://farnamstreetblog.com, in a weekly e-mail newsletter called Brain Food;

Investment Masters Class, website at https://mastersinvest.com/investmentuniversity/ and e-mails.

For old-fashioned book learning, I invite you to peruse the bibliography.

Conclusion

Well, that's it. That's what I know right now.

Nutshell version: work hard all your life; invest at least 10 percent of what you earn—no arguments—from the get-go, preferably in tax-deferred or nontaxable Roth retirement accounts using low-cost index funds invested in US stocks; always live well within your means; debt is for home mortgages and education only.

Oh, and marry once, carefully, for keeps. Divorce is very expensive. Admiration-based love is best. Obsessive love is bad. Romantic, well...

Never buy luxury cars. Get quality preowned cars or trucks. Drive them unto the auto graveyard and mourn them well.

Buy the sweetest, most modest house in the best neighborhood you can afford.

Avoid litigation.

Take care of your health.

Beware of any and all addictions, including substances, Internet, sex, risk, and gambling.

When you have an insoluble problem invert, always invert.

Follow Charlie Munger's fundamental algorithm of life: *repeat what works!*

And the corollary: *stop what doesn't work!*

Remember George Bailey and the compounded virtues of a life well led.

And have a wonderful life.

Bibliography

Barkow, Jerome H., Leda Cosmides, and John Tooby. *The Adapted Mind: Evolutionary Psychology and the Generation of Culture.* Oxford: Oxford University Press, 1992.

Bevelin, Peter S. *All I Want to Know is Where I'm Going to Die So I'll Never Go There: Buffett and Munger—A Study in Simplicity and Uncommon, Common Sense.* Glendale, CA: PCA Publications, 2016.

Bevelin, Peter S. *Seeking Wisdom: From Darwin to Munger.* 3rd ed. Glendale, CA: PCA Publications, 2007.

Bogle, John C. *The Little Book of Common Sense Investing: The Only Way to Guarantee Your Fair Share of Market Returns.* New York: Wiley, 2007.

Cialdini, Robert B. *Influence: The Psychology of Persuasion.* New York: Harper Business, 2006.

Clark, David. *Tao of Charlie Munger: A Compilation of Quotes from Berkshire Hathaway's Vice Chairman on Life, Business and the Pursuit of Wealth with Commentary by David Clark.* New York: Scribner & Sons, 2017.

Clason, George S. *The Richest Man in Babylon.* New York: Signet, 1988.

Darwin, Charles. *The Origin of the Species.* New York: Bantam, 1999.

DeLaVega, Jose. *Confusion de confusiones.* Eastford, CT: Martino Fine Books, 2013.

Duhigg, Charles. *The Power of Habit: Why We Do What We Do in Life and Business.* New York: Random House Trade Paperback, 2014.

Freud, Sigmund. *Group Psychology and the Analysis of the Ego.* New York: W. W. Norton & Co., 1990.

Graham, Benjamin, *The Intelligent Investor*. Revised Edition. New York: Harper, 2006.

Graham, Benjamin, and David Dodd. *Security Analysis*. New York: McGraw-Hill Education, 2008.

Griffin, Tren. *Charlie Munger: The Complete Investor*. New York: Columbia Business School Publishing, 2015.

Isaacson, Walter. *Einstein: His Life and Universe*. New York: Simon & Schuster, 2008.

Kahneman, Daniel. *Thinking, Fast and Slow*. New York: Farrar, Straus and Giroux, 2011.

Kaufman, Peter D., ed. *Poor Charlie's Almanack: The Wit and Wisdom of Charles T. Munger*. Expanded Third Edition. Marcelline, MO: Walsworth Publishing Company, 2005.

LeBon, Gustave. *The Crowd: A Study of the Popular Mind*. North Charleston, SC: CreateSpace Independent Publishing Platform, 2012.

Lewis, Michael. *The Undoing Project: A Friendship That Changed Our Minds*. New York: W. W. Norton & Company, 2016.

Lowe, Janet. *Damn Right! Behind the Scenes with Berkshire Hathaway Billionaire Charlie Munger*. New York: John Wiley & Sons, 2000.

Machiavelli, Niccolo. *The Prince*. North Charleston, SC: CreateSpace Independent Publishing Platform, 2014.

Mackay, Charles. *Extraordinary Popular Delusions and the Madness of Crowds*. North Charleston, SC: CreateSpace Independent Publishing Platform, 2013.

Malkiel, Burton G. *A Random Walk Down Wall Street: The Time-Tested Strategy for Successful Investing*. New York: W. W. Norton & Company, 2016.

Marks, Howard. *The Most Important Thing: Uncommon Sense for the Thoughtful Investor*. New York: Columbia Business School Publishing, 2011.

Miller, Jeremy C. *Warren Buffett's Ground Rules: Words of Wisdom from the Partnership Letters of the World's Greatest Investor*. New York: Harper Business, 2016.

Nofsinger, John R. *The Psychology of Investing*. Abingdon: Routledge, 2017.

O'Shaughnessy, James P. *What Works on Wall Street*. 4th ed. New York: McGraw-Hill, 2012.

Pecaut, Daniel, and Corey Wrenn. *University of Berkshire Hathaway: 30 Years of Lessons Learned from Warren Buffett & Charlie Munger at the Annual Shareholders Meeting*. Sioux City: Pecaut & Co., 2017.

Schroeder, Alice. *The Snowball: Warren Buffett and the Business of Life*. New York: Bantam Books, 2008.

Schwed, Fred. *Where Are The Customers' Yachts?: Or, a Good Hard Look at Wall Street*. New York: Wiley, 2006.

Smith, Adam. *The Wealth of Nations*. New York: Bantam Classics, 2003.

Stanley, Thomas J., and William D. Danko. *The Millionaire Next Door*. New York: Gallery Books, 1998.

Taleb, Nassim Nicholas, *Fooled by Randomness: The Hidden role of Chance in Life and in the Markets*, New York: Random House, 2008.

Zweig, Jason. *The Devil's Financial Dictionary*. New York: Public Affairs, 2015.

About the Author

Mark Tobak, MD, is a general adult psychiatrist in private practice. He is the former chief of inpatient geriatric psychiatry at St. Vincent's Hospital in Harrison, New York, where he is an attending physician.

Dr. Tobak graduated the University at Buffalo School of Medicine after receiving a pre-medical certificate from the Columbia University School of General Studies. Before pursuing a career in medicine, Dr. Tobak received his law degree from Fordham University School of Law and was admitted to the New York State Bar.

Dr. Tobak's work has been published in the *American Journal of Psychiatry*, *Psychiatric Times*, and the *American Journal of Medicine and Pathology*. He is the author of *Anyone Can Be Rich!* and *Audio Alternative: The Definitive Guide to High Fidelity*.